Reproduced by kind permission of The Guildhall Library.

Arethusa, Lady Harland's Commonplace Book

Arethusa, Lady Harland, aged 58
Oil, 30 by 25 ins, attributed to John Whitehead Walton

MEMORANDUMS

of

VARIOUS SORTS

made between 1827 and 1833

by

ARETHUSA

LADY HARLAND

at

Orwell Park

and

Richmond Terrace

Lady Harland
Began this Book
January 1827

Moore Mackay Publishing Ltd.
1992

© Moore Mackay Publishing Ltd.
190 Strand, London WC2R 1JN

ISBN 0 9520221 0 9

Printed and bound in Great Britain by
Biddles Ltd, Guildford and King's Lynn

The cover illustration of Miss Arethusa Vernon is from a miniature, 3 by $2\frac{1}{2}$ ins, signed P. Paillou, 1796. Both portraits of Arethusa, from the Cullum Collection, are reproduced by kind permission of St Edmundsbury Borough Council.

CONTENTS

ILLUSTRATIONS

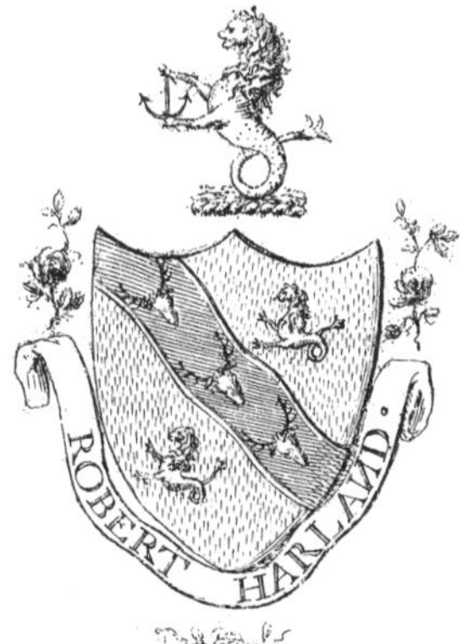
ROBERT HARLAND

FOREWORD

One might expect a great niece of 'Old Grog' Vernon to be launched with a name like Arethusa, but she was only following her paternal grandmother, a daughter of Lord Clifford; a sister-in-law of the Admiral can hardly have been named in his honour. Our Arethusa's mother was a daughter of Sir John Cullum, 5th Baronet, her uncle the Earl of Shipbrooke. In 1801, aged 24, she married Sir Robert Harland, son of Admiral Sir Robert of Sproughton whom he succeeded in the baronetcy in 1784. With Robert and Arethusa the lines of Vernon and Harland both came to an end, but together they enjoyed the many Suffolk estates which came to them from their families at Wherstead, Nacton, Great Thurlow, Hundon and a dozen other parishes, some dispersed in sales in 1811 and 1820.

The Harlands' first home was Wherstead Park, just south of Ipswich and high (for Suffolk) above the Orwell. The estate had been purchased by Sir Robert's widowed mother in 1791, but in 1814 an exchange for that of Orwell Park across the river at Nacton was agreed with Arethusa's brother, John Vernon, heir of Francis Vernon, Earl of Shipbrooke. The Harlands found tenants for Wherstead Park when four years later it became theirs again on the death of John Vernon. For a London residence they chose Number 3 Richmond Terrace, just across Whitehall from Downing Street, in those days with a splendid view of the Thames. Thomas Chawner was the architect; building took from 1822 until 1825, and the Harlands set themselves up there in 1828. At first they hired houses at Felixstowe for the summer, but as the resort was becoming increasingly fashionable, they built a handsome villa for occasional residence there in 1843. They also holidayed in France and the Channel Islands, sometimes setting sail in their own craft from the Orwell to do so.

The Harlands lived for 33 years at Orwell Park, but when in 1847 the estate was sold to Colonel Tomline, they returned to Wherstead where Sir Robert died the following August and was buried in a vault in the churchyard. When in 1860 Arethusa was laid to rest beside him, her coffin plate was inscribed 'the last of the Vernons of Great Thurlow'. Arethusa put up a mural memorial to Sir Robert in the church, its inscription evidently but inexplicably altered. They share an 'Acts of Mercy' west window in the tower, the work of William Holland of Warwick.

With so many naval connections, who better than Arethusa Lady

Harland to do the honours at a ship launch. In the *Ipswich Journal* for Saturday the 29th September 1821 we read:

'Thursday last another beautiful vessel, of 1350 tons, intended for the East India Trade, was launched from Mr Jabez Bayley's ship yard in this town. At about 12 o'clock Lady Harland, who had been solicited to perform the ceremony of naming her, supported by Rear Admiral Page and Joseph Hare Esq the managing owner, and accompanied by Lord and Lady Granville and a party of fashionables went to the ship, when her Ladyship with great grace and spirit exclaimed, "May God bless the good ship William Fairlie;" this was followed by hearty cheers and about 1/4 past 12 the ship entered her proper element in grand stile. At one, having cleared the Dock, the Swift steam packet took her in tow, and with this aid she glided majestically down the river.'

It is interesting that Arethusa had the company of the Granvilles at the ceremony, for only three weeks earlier Sir Robert Harland had heavily defeated the Blue party nominee for the High Stewardship of the Borough, none other than the Duke of Wellington. Never before had there been a contest for this august and honorary office; it had been held between 1800 and his death by Nelson. That the Granvilles would have supported the Iron Duke goes without saying, for he was their guest at Wherstead Park during a visit to Ipswich the previous January when he was granted the Honorary Freedom of the Borough.

Arethusa enjoyed 47 years of marriage to Sir Robert and lived a dozen more his widow, but we have no way of knowing how much she and Sir Robert (as she always referred to him even in her own Memorandum Book) regretted that they had no offspring, no direct heirs. Few Harland archives have survived, certainly nothing extensive in the way of letters and diaries. For that reason if for none other it is worth reproducing this slight compilation, the fortunate discovery of one who has made many such in a Guildford bookshop long a favourite haunt of the finder and owner, Brian Moore, and of the Editor's. Lady Harland's text is transcribed *verbatim*, retaining her idiosyncracies of spelling and punctuation in English and in French. Her entries are numbered consecutively to aid indexing.

The memoranda have several endearing characteristics of their collector. First, Arethusa might well have subtitled her book 'Recommendations by Persons of Taste'; the opening entry shows how anxious Arethusa was to be reminded that the great and the good had placed their *imprimatur* on tradespeople, remedies and recipes:

'Hadfield's Tincture for Sprains, Bruises, &c. &c. sent to Sir Robert by Captn. Wollaston to whom it was given by Lady Surrey.'

Secondly, we see how, once her duties as mistress of Orwell Park were carried out (always meticulously, as poor Lyon must have found as supplies of candles ran out too quickly), Lady Harland's thoughts and fingers ran in pursuit of the decorative arts. Her name appears on a printed list of 'distinguished pupils' of Henry Bright, but that can be no measure of her skill at drawing. Perhaps some who read about her hobbies may identify surviving examples of her work. Memorandum 109 perhaps states her ruling maxim in just two lines:

> Seek to be good, aim not to be great
> A Womans noblest station is retreat.

John Blatchly
Ipswich 1992

WHERSTEAD LODGE, SUFFOLK, *the Residence of the* RT. HON. VISCT. GRANVILLE.

INDEX BY SUBJECTS

The numbers below refer to the memoranda which have been numbered consecutively

Engraving of Orwell Park by T. Barber after J.P. Neale, published 1st June 1822 in the latter's Views of the Seats.

RECOMMENDATIONS BY PERSONS OF TASTE

Alloway, Mrs, probably housekeeper at Richmond Terrace 85, 87
Angerstein, Mrs, wife of John Angerstein, Esq. of Weeting Hall, Brandon 9
Anson, Lady 75
Arcedeckne, Mrs, wife of Andrew Arcedeckne, Esq. of Glevering Hall, Hacheston 68
Berners, Mr Charles, of Woolverstone Park 100
Berners, Mrs Henry Denny, wife of Archdeacon Berners of the same 198
Blessington, Lady, 2nd wife of the 2nd Earl 112
Blois, Sir Charles and Lady, of Cockfield Hall, Yoxford133, 161
Calvert, Charles, M.P. for Southwark 81, 193 *(obit.)*
Campbell, Mr and Mrs William Frederick, of Birkfield, Ipswich 86, 87
Clanricard, Marchioness 143
Cleveland, 1st Marquess of, 60
Cooper, Sir Astley, of Hemel Hempstead 105
Coutt[s?], Mr 147
Cullum, Sir Thomas Gery and Lady, of Hardwick House, Hawstead 19, 80
Cullum, Mrs, possibly the wife of James, Rector of Nacton 1787-1835 182, 190
Cuthbert, Miss 74
Euston, Countess of 146
FitzGerald, Miss Jane, sister or dau. of John FitzGerald, Esq., tenant of Wherstead Park 1825-35 175
Fludyer, Miss, dau. or sister of Sir Samuel Fludyer of Felixstowe Lodge 82
Garrett, Mr 61
Granville, 1st Viscount and Viscountess, tenant of Wherstead Park 1819-25, from 1833 4th Earl and Countess 12, 13, 55
Harland, Lady, Dowager of Admiral Harland who died 1784 86
Kilderbee, Miss, daughter of Samuel Kilderbee, Esq. of Framlingham and Ipswich 141
Martin, Lady 9, 103, 119, 145, 146
Martin, Mr, Mrs and Miss, of Hemingstone Hall 69, 70, 102, 105, 119
Merest, Mrs, wife of the Revd. J.W.D. Merest, of Bury St Edmunds in 1827, presented to living of Cockfield with Staindrop, Co. Durham by Lord Cleveland in 1829 7, 62, 65
Methold, Mrs, wife of the Revd. Thomas Methold, Rector of Stonham Aspal since 1789 124

ROBERT HARLAND.

PEDIGREES OF HARLAND AND VERNON

HARLAND

Capt. Robert Harland R.N.

Adm. Sir Robert Harland, Bt*
of Sproughton, cr. 1771
C-in-C E.I.Fleet, 2 i/c to
Admiral Keppel, d. 1784

VERNON

Admiral Edward Vernon
M.P. for Ipswich 1740-57

James Vernon
m. Arethusa, dau.
of Ld. Clifford

Henry
Gt Thurlow
Hall

= Jane Cullum
dau of Sir John,
5th Bt.

Francis, Baron,
Visct. Orwell,
E. of Shipbrooke
d. 1783

1801
Sir ROBERT HARLAND, Bt = ARETHUSA
1765-1848 1777-1860
Both d.s.p.

John
d.1818

1. Frances, wife of the Edward, 13th Viscount Dillon, whose daughter was Countess Karolyi

2. Marianne-Dorothy, wife of Major-Genl. the Hon. Wm. Dalrymple, mother of the 7th Earl of Stair

3. Susannah Edith, wife of Sir Wm. Rowley of Tendring Hall

---

*Adm. Harland m. the dau. of Col Rowland Reynold, gd-dau. & heiress of Col. John Duncombe

MEMORANDUMS OF VARIOUS SORTS

Hadfield's Tincture for Sprains, Bruises, &c. &c. sent to Sir Robert by Captn Wollaston to whom it was given by Lady Surrey.
8 Tea spoonfuls of the best double proof Brandy
6 Do of Rectified Spirits of Wine
1oz of Castille Soap
1oz of Potash
2 Drachms of double refined Sugar

Scrape the Soap fine & dissolve both that and the Sugar in the Spirits then add the Potash & mix them entirely by shakeing. Let it stand two days & then decant it from the Dregs through brown paper, keep it close stopped up from the Air.

2
Almacks Novel
Lady Birmingham supposed to be Mrs Beaumont
Lady Lochaber — Lady Keith
Duchess of Stavordale — Bedford
The Lady with gawky daughters – Sefton

3
Receipt to make Ink (Col. Rigby's *1819*)
Two ounces of Gall nuts bruized small
One do. of Copperas, clear, rocky & green
One do. of Gum Arabic
a Quarter of an ounce of Rock Allum in a Pint of Soft Water. Let the above stand in a Stone bottle, shake it well once a day, exposing it to the air for ten days, then add a glass of Brandy to prevent it from getting mouldy.

4
1826
Le Sage, Rue Grange Bateliere, an Upholsterer at Paris recommended by Mr Middleton.

Le Vacher, Duke of Devonshire's Upholsterer opposite the Café Larde.

5
1826
Hotel de Bristol, Place Vendôme, much recommended by Mr & Mrs Middleton. Kept by an Englishwoman.

6
Advertisement
To Invalids – Exercising Chamber Horses.
Hope of Rathbone Place Oxford Street London embraces this opportunity of returning his grateful thanks to the Gentlemen of the faculty who have so confidently recommended this truly useful Machine, the properties of which far surpass any thing hitherto invented for the amusement & exercise of persons labouring under maladies which require gentle or active exertion. By the use of the hands, the afflicted are capable of taking exercise as pleasant as on the most gentle, or equal to a trotting horse, & by its powers, it causes genial warmth & general circulation of the blood. The Springs are so tempered as to carry from six to twenty stone or more. They are in price from eight to 12 Guineas agreable to the weight they are intended to carry, or may be hired. Likewise an Improved Leg-rest, which no one should be without who is subject to gout, rheumatism, cold or damp feet. Bath, Merlin, & Invalid chairs bought or exchanged.

7
1826
Mrs Merest told me of a Mrs Groves a Widow who lives in No. 41 Jermyn Street, which house is just new built & new furnished, the old one being burnt down last year. She has excellent Lodgings to lett & has a good Cook &c. – it is a good place to go to for a night or two or longer, instead of an Hotel. She cooks what you order, & it is the same as if you kept house yourself.

8

From London to Hockerill	– 30 miles
on to Saffron Walden	13
on to Haverhill	13
	56

From Hundon through Clare to Braintree, to Ingatestone, to Romford, & to London, total 55 miles.

Haverhill is	4 miles from Clare
Hundon	3 miles from Clare
Clare	14 miles from Bury

From Haverhill to Linton	9 miles
From Linton to Cambridge	11 Do.

From Orwell to Hadleigh	15 miles
On to Melford	12 Do.
On to Clare	9 Do.
On to Hundon	3 Do.

From Thurlow, through Little Thurlow go on to Great Bradley (which is about a mile & a half from Great Thurlow), & opposite the Public House to the right the road leads to Cowling (commonly called Coolidge); about 3 miles from Cowling in the same direction is Lidgate, & 3 miles further on is Dalham. Cowlinge *i.e.* about 5 miles from Gt. Thurlow.

9
Perfumes for Bags &c.

Esterhazy's Bouquet – prepared by Bailey & Blews, Cockspur Street, Charing Cross, London.

Vitivert is an excellent Perfume, an Essence Muguet Do. – these two to be had at Del Croixs, perfumer in Bond St.
Sachez Powder at Gallies, perfumer, Bond St. for perfumed Bags and Peau d'Espagne – a Perfumed skin it retains the Smell longer than any thing – Lady Martin says it is Mrs Angerstein's Perfume, &c. &c. perfumed bags.

10
E Sparhall   Drabbet Manufacturer   Haverhill Suffolk

Miss Ann Abbott – now Mrs Speller – Corset Maker – No. 4 Wigmore Street Cavendish Square – London – from Mrs Baileys, Holles Street.

11
Pattersons Ice Pail, on a perfectly new & philosophical principle, by means of which Wines, Butter, Cream, fruit &c. may be cooled & kept cool with a degree of efficacy & precision hitherto unknown. Pattersons Ice Bucket for preserving Ice for several days.

12
Snow Boots
Thomas Roper – St Peters – Ipswich – at the foot of the Bridge – he made several for Ld. Granville

13
Shooting Boots
Mr Roe – Ipswich – made for Ld. Glle.

14
Beer – Brewing
The art of brewing is exactly similar to the process of making Tea – Put a handful of Malt into a Tea Pot, then fill it with water, the first time rather under boiling heat; after it has stood some time, pour off the Liquor, just as you would Tea, and fill up the pot again with boiling water, in a similar manner pour that off till the Malt in the pot is tasteless, which will be the case when all the virtue is extracted.
The Liquor or Malt Tea thus extracted must then be boiled with a few Hops in it, and when it becomes cool enough, that is, about blood heat, add a little yeast to ferment it, and the thing is done.
This is the whole art & process of Brewing & to brew a larger quantity requires just the same mode of proceeding as it would to make a Tea Breakfast for a Regiment of Soldiers – A Peck of Malt & four ounces of Hops will produce ten quarts of Ale, better than any that can be puchased in London, & for which purpose a tea kettle and two pan mugs are sufficient apparatus. Mechanics Magazine
copied from Morning Herald *Septbr. 1826*

15
One of the Pictures drawn by Col. Bunbury & Mr Charles Tyrrel – an etching – was for Denny Fuller – an old Shoe Maker in Bury that used to be called the Lady Killer – he always wore a satin Waistcoat on a Sunday – quite a character. Also by the same an Etching of the Old Bury Newsman by name Robinson who used to cry the Bury Newspapers about the streets on a Wednesday – also an Etching of Billy Barbrook a Travelling Tinker in Bury who carried so many things of his trade about him.

16
1826
Churchills Treatise on Acupuncturation – he lives at No. 13 Princes Street, Leicester Square & is a Surgeon.

James Scott, Esqr. (Surgeon) No. 30 Newington Causeway – London – & Editor of the Journal of Public Health – was the first person who introduced Acupuncturation into England – it is an operation of introducing a needle from an Inch & 1/2 to Two Inches into the Flesh – it is not at all painfull & performs wonderful cures in wandering Rheumatism, Lumbago & Sciatica &c.

Denny Fuller *Shoemaker*

Tilly Ling *Hot gingerbread & mutton pies*

Robinson *Newsman*

Robert Martin *Matches & Almanacks*

Bury Characters etched by Henry Bunbury

Edward Jukes Esqr. (surgeon) Terrace, Pimlico, is successful in cases of Acupuncturation.

The Publication above alluded to, is a description of a surgical operation, originally peculiar to the Japanese & Chinese, & by them denominated Zin-King, now introduced into European practice, with the directions for its performance, and cases illustrating its success. By James Morse Churchill, Fellow of the Royal College of Surgeons, in London Octavo pp.86 with Plates. Mr Jukes improved needles are what are used.

17
The Journal of Public Health; or Family Guide to Medicine – explaining the nature & effects of Natural & philosophical Phenomena of Diet, of Medicine, & Regimen, & of Domestic Economy, with directions to the Sick and the Healthy, the young & the infirm and the aged for restoring & preserving health.

By James Scott, Esqr., Surgeon &c. &c., London, printed for the Editor & published by Messrs. Sherwood, Jones & Co., Paternoster Row – 1823 – Sold by all Booksellers.

18
1823
Asylum for the Recovery of Health.
An Institution lately established in Gower St., New Road, London, for those living on narrow incomes, & well educated persons reduced by the casualties of life who would have prompt & various succour which they could not obtain at their own dwellings.
The sick Members also of the families of many respectable artizans & mechanics, clerks on small salaries, apprentices, domestics of the higher Class & of irreproachable character would be glad to avail themselves of such a resource. For besides lodging & diet they would have the benefit of experienced nurses, resident medical officers, a store of medicine &c. Another important object of the establishment is of recovering persons afflicted by protracted disease, requiring for their cure perhaps twelve-months confinement or more to their Beds, & consequently improper cases for public Hospitals. Terms of admission are that any person applying must have a letter of recommendation signed by a Governor & are to pay the weekly sum of 12 Shillings for Females, 14 Shillings for Males, & from 7 to 10 Shillings for Children.

19
Kaleidoscope
Lady Cullum had a long narrow China Jar made into a Kaleidoscope, it was her own idea & I thought it a good one. It was done by an Optician of the name of Bancks – 441 Strand, London.

20
Biscuits
Trapnell – Baker at Coddenham nr. Ipswich for the thin Hard Biscuits which are so excellent.

21
1826
Patent Side Saddles which were invented last Spring & gave such universal satisfaction, can only be had at Mr Peats, saddler, 167 Piccadilly & at Mr Barretts Riding School, Cheltenham.

22
Piping Bull Finches & Canaries
Von Der Hullen has just arrived from High Germany with a fine collection of piping Bullfinches which pipe Malbrook, Going Colin, Marches, Waltzes & country dances – also a great variety of German Canaries which sing the Nightingale & Titlark notes – are to be sold at 25 St Martin's Lane, Charing Cross, on the first floor at Mr Stockham's, boot tree, & French Clog Manufacturers

23
Gentlemens Elastic Belts – 65 New Bond St – by Robinson & Visitern

24
1826
Extensive Stock of Millinery at Mrs Mealings, 56 Wigmore Street – every thing new & splendid in Hats & Bonnets appropriate to the Season, Silver & Gold Head Dresses, Blond Lace & French worked Caps – Leghorn Hats & Bonnets, Turbans & Capotes in great variety – Prices full 50 per cent under other houses, for Ready Money only,

25
The Game of the Conjuror

The Box to be closed immediately the conjuror is put in.

The White Conjuror is very light in weight

The Green	Do	loaded & very heavy
The Red	Do	moves in the Box
The Yellow	Do	moves not
The Black	Do	heavy & dull having Mercury inside which moves as it is shaken

From Howell & James 9 Regent St *6th July 1827*

26
1826

Mrs Thomas Holding
(Artist. Sister of Mr Bullock, of the Museum, Piccadilly.)
and her daughters

respectfully solicit the Ladies to view their elegant specimens of Embossed Velvet, and Rice Paper, on Jars, Vases &c. Artificial Fruit and Flowers, Painting on Satin, Velvet, Wood, and Glass: Chinese Imitation of Inlaid Mother of Pearl, Coral &c.
On a principle so accurate and easily acquired that Mrs T.H. will pledge herself to make any Pupil perfect Mistress of either of the Arts in one Lesson. Terms one Guinea each Art.
Ladies favouring Mrs T.H. with a Trial will not find themselves led into the expenses for materials, generally the case with professional persons. The Money for Instructions to be paid on the receipt of each separate Art. Specimens of the above (in the acquisitions of which the Rudiments of Drawing are quite unnecessary) together with a variety of Gold and Silver Flowers, Trimmings for Court and Ball Dresses in the most superb style on sale, are always ready for inspection at their Establishment, 49, Wigmore St., Cavendish Square, within twenty miles of which, Mrs. T.H. will attend any family free of extra charge, having a conveyance for that purpose.

Note. Mrs Holding is removed to Bond St.

27
For Palpitations and Head Aches

Three grains of Rhubarb & a Grain of Ipecacuanha to be made into Two Pills & to be taken before Breakfast. Dr Baillies Prescription to Lady Rous.

Note. Sir Robt. tried this Prescription and did not like it, he thought it made him feel sick.

28
A list of Newspapers sent by Mr Barrow, Clerk of the Ipswich Road General Post Office, London.

Evening Papers published daily, are the Courier, Globe, Sun, Star.
Those published three times per week are the St James's Chronicle and the English Chronicle, every Tuesday, Thursday & Saturday.
The London Packet & The Evening Mail, every Monday, Wednesday & Friday.

29
From London to Orwell.

White Hart, Romford, where Horses were ordered between 11 & 12.

Ingatestone	one o'clock.
Blue Post, Witham	½ past Two.
Colchester	Four.
Copdock	qr. after Five.

30
For making Flowers.
In dyeing Roses, put your strips of Muslin in Water with Lemon Juice, before they are dyed in the middle.
Red, Pink. Saucer with Lemon juice, put your Muslin into it hot for some minutes.
Crimson. Carmine Powder with Spirits of wine.
Blue Flowers, use Smalt.
In Scarlet Geraniums, dye your Muslin Yellow, then paint them with Carmine.
To colour Stalk. Paper, sap green dissolved in Water, & sponged over tissue Paper.

Liquids.

Blue	Scotts Blue.
Yellow	1 Gill of spirits of Wine ½oz Turmeric.

Seeds.

Yellow	Semolina – if Semolina cannot be had, then Ground Rice.
Green	mix a little Yellow and Blue Liquid with Semolina.
Brown	Ground Coffee.

31
Moores Patent Typographical Instruments for marking on Linen, Silk, Woollen &c. by the pressure of the Hand only with Ink warranted Indelible. These Instruments are very portable and extremely durable. They are recommended to the Officers of the Army, &c. by the Commander His Royal Highness the Duke of York in general Orders issued from the Horse Guards 18th of Janry. 1812. Coat of Arms, Devices, Autographs &c. engraved in Brass or Wood for marking on Linen, for Gilding on Books, Paper, &c.
Manufactured & sold by T. Moore patentee & Inventor at the sign of the Golden {A} removed from Drury Lane to 84 Quadrant, Regent St. near Piccadilly, London.

32
Useful discovery – A Correspondent of the Stamford Bee says "I have by Accident discovered what might be useful to some of your readers to know – that the clear solution of chloride of Lime, diluted with twice its bulk of water will effectually & expeditiously remove stains from Prints and printed paper. Instead of the ordinary process which is expensive & tedious, first soak the print in clear water till it lies smooth; then remove it into a dish large enough to hold it flat, filled up with the solution diluted as above: the stains will disappear in a few minutes when again soak the Print in clear water, to free it from the chloride of Lime, and then dry it between sheets of blotting paper. By this process I have bleached 12 Prints and letter press belonging to an expensive book which had been damaged by rain and sea water."

33
Those who invited us to dinner *May 1826* when at Thomas's Hotel

Sir Wm. Rowley	6th accepted
Mr Arcedeckne	7th accepted
Mrs Joseph Smith	12th accepted
Mr Wilbraham	13th Sir Robt accepted
Mrs Rowley	15th not accepted
Mr Garrett	15th Sir Robt accepted
Sir Charles & Lady Rowley	15th not accepted
Mrs Vernon	16th accepted
Mr Fitzgerald	18th accepted
Mr Langford Brook	18th not accepted
Mr Adair	20th not accepted – both invited
Sir Wm. Rowley	20th not accepted
Mr Middleton	22nd Do.

Sir Charles & Lady Ibbotson	Do. Do.
Mr Arcedeckne	24th accepted
Sir Samuel Fludyer	25th Do.
Mrs Vernon	26th Do.
Sir Thomas & Lady Lennard	27th not accepted
Ld. Rochford	Do. Sir Robt accepted
Sir Richard & Lady King	29th accepted
Mr Dickinson	1st of June not accepted as we left town

Invited *June ye 5th* to a Quadrille Ball at 9 o'clock at Mrs John Wrights – Bellesize Park – Hampstead

Lady Astley at Home – Monday *May ye 15th* – we were invited before to Lady Astley but did not go.

34
List of the Men Sir Robt. called on

Lt Genl Sir Wm. Pringle
Col. Gibbs
Col. Sir Charles Br. Vere
Lt Col Mercer
Mr G.J. Philip Smith
Mr Leveson Gower
Ld. Carrington
Mr Waddington
Sir Thos. Lennard

Mr Lumley
Mr Bazley
Mr John Berners
Mr Coke
Sir Richd. King
Mr Francis Beckford junr.
Earl of Euston
Sir Charles Rowley
Major Broke
Sir T.G. Cullum

Mr Horace Beckford
Mr Pettiward
Sir Saml. Fludyer
Sir Jacob Astley
Mr Middleton
Sir Wm. Anson
Earl of Rochford
Mr John James Smith
Sir St Vincent Cotton
Sir Thos. Hammond
Sir Edwd. Kerrison
Mr Walter Arcedeckne

Mr Langford Brooke
Col. Armstrong
Mr Henry Martin
Mr W.C. Smith
Mr Letwin
Mr Wilbraham
Mr E. Leveson Gower
Mr Scourfield
Earl of Stradbroke
Ld. Charles Fitzroy senr.

Mr Dickinson
Earl of Albemarle
Sir Henry Peyton
Mr Fitzgerald
Sir Charles Ibbotson
Mr Edmund Byng
Revd. Alexander Cotton
Mr Barnardiston
Sir Edwd. Codrington
Ld. Charles Fitzroy, Burlington House

35

Isinglass Jelly – to strengthen

2oz of Isinglass boiled in a pint of Water till reduced to ½ a pint – then add a small bit of cinnamon, a Bay leaf or two, and a small bit of Lemon Peel – boil it up again & then strain it off – either add a glass of Sherry to it when strained or when you melt it which is done by putting a small quantity into a Wineglass & set it in hot water – to a Wine-glass add a teaspoonful of Sherry.

36

Those that I called on in *1829* & that returned it

Mrs & Miss Powell
Mrs Arcedeckne
Mr Douglas Mercer
Lady Astley & Miss Astley
Mrs Rigby
Miss Mercer
Mrs John Wright
Mrs T. Dickins
Lady Ann Coke
Mrs Rowley & Miss Wade
Lady Ibbotson
Mrs Barnardiston senr.
Mrs Henry Martin
Lady Kerrison
Mrs Joseph Smith
Honble. Mrs & 2 Miss Calverts
Mrs & 2 Miss Fitzgeralds
Lady Jane Bayly
Countess of Carlisle
Mrs Scourfield
Mrs Selwyn
Mrs Charles Calvert
Mrs Horace George Broke
Mrs Beckford
Mrs Verdon
Lady Codrington
Marchioness & the Ladies Cornwallis
Dowager Lady Brownslow & Miss Custs
Countess of Albemarle
Lady Peyton
Mrs Langford Brooke
Lady Charles Rowley
Countess of Stradbroke
Mrs Botham
Mrs Waddington
Mrs Henry Dawkins & Miss Dawkins
Lady Barrett Lennard & Miss Lennard
Julia Lady Petre & 2 Miss Petres

37

1829 the following were prescribed by Dr Bernard of Clifton & Lady Middleton wrote them down & sent them to me.

For a relaxed Sore Throat

Scrape some Horse radish fine, & pour some boiling water upon it, till it become a comfortable strength, then add to it a spoonful of White Wine Vinegar & a tea spoonful of Honey, and apply it as a Gargle now & then, but not constantly.

To remove the unpleasant feel after Inflamation of the Trachea
One part of Lime Water & two of Milk to be used as a Gargle night & morning.

38
Mrs H. Hainsworth
Hill House Bank
Leeds
Yorkshire

Mrs Buffinin's Mothers direction

39
The Pocket Book called, The Regent, or Rahal Tablet of Memory which I had in 1820 seems the best I ever saw – it contained an Almanack, a variety of useful Information & twelve views of Gentlemen's seats and Monuments &c. continued annually.
Printed for John Poole, No. 48 Fetter Lane & Hodgsons – Wimpole St. & various others

40
Quinine Bark
or New French Bark
A Cure for the Ague
Gall the Chymist at Bury sells Boxes of Pills made of the above Bark – Dr Probert of Bury says 3 Doses of the Bark will cure 9 people out of twelve of the Ague.

41
Beer
Lyons Statement *March 1827*

To make One Hogshead of Ale, & 1 of Small Beer

2 Comb of Malt at 28/ per Co.	2 = 16 = 0
8 lbs of Hops at one shilling per lb	0 = 8 = 0
	£3 = 4 = 0

The above will answer equally well for 2 Hogsheads of Table Beer

1 Hogshead of Ale – 54 Gallons at 6d a quart, 2/ a Gallon	5 = 8 = 0
1 Hogshead of small Beer suppose 1½d a quart – 6d a Gallon	1 = 7 = 0
The Common Brewer	6 = 15 = 0
The Private Brewer	3 = 4 = 0
There remains	£3 = 11 = 0 in favour

of the private Brewer exclusive of its greater superiority.

42
The famous Woman for all sorts of fancy Work for Ladies is Mrs Bryden (late Smallwood) 5 Little Maddox Street – Bond St London *April 1827*

43
Quilters House – Felixstow
2 Sitting Rooms, 3 best Bed Rooms, 2 Attics one of them with 2 Servts. Beds the other for a Ladies Maid – 2 Cellars – Earthen Ware & all that is wanted for use in the Kitchen – for 4 Guineas a week. There is another part of the House that is lett separately consisting of a small room below paved with pamments which I suppose is used as a sort of Kitchen, 2 Best Bed Rooms one of which has a Press Bedstead that it may be used as a Sitting Room, 2 Attics one of them with 2 Beds – this is lett for 2 Guineas, but if you take the whole house you may have it for 5 Guineas a week. There is also a Bakehouse & Scullery which we did not use – the best end of the House has two Stair Cases.
The person who has the care of it keeps a little Shop close to it & you may direct to her Mrs Franks, High Row, Felixstow.
Mrs Porter keeps the other Lodging House.

44
1828 April ye 6th Sir Robert wrote to Mr Callaghan, Banker at Paris, to request him to pay Monsr. Le Sage, 15,383 francs for furniture & 815 francs for a Carpet which Le Sage would pay the Manufacturer for – also 4235 francs to Messrs Fournier & Julmasse for the 2 large Drawing Room Carpets or Rugs. Total 20,433 francs – about 818£ English money.

1250 francs were then 50£ Sterling

Drawn by Thos. H. Shepherd. Engraved by M. S. Barenger.

RICHMOND TERRACE, WHITEHALL.

TO R. WILMOT HORTON, ESQ. M.P. &c. &c. THIS PLATE IS RESPECTFULLY INSCRIBED.

The Carpets were called Tapis Veloutes of the Aubusson Manufactory. The large one with Brown Ground we [paid] 70 francs the Square yard which is Ell in England from Fournier & Julmasse.
The Green Ground in the Boudoir was 80 francs the yard & bought of another manufacturer.
Mr Le Sage the Upholsterer in Paris furnished our three Rooms on Richmond Terrace, Whitehall, & they were done much handsomer & with considerable less expense than if it had been done by English Upholsterers, duty & carriage, & every expense included – the Couches and Chairs covered with Lyons Silk – & the Walls all covered with french Silk.

The French Writing Table was charged	210 francs
The Ecarté Table	180 Do.
The Flower Vases on Chimney Piece	300 Do.

45
Odell Burlington Arcade, London, is the place where you can get Gold Lace for trimming cloaks &c. &c. – it is a Military Shop I believe – recommended to me.

46
Pomme de Calvin is the French Desert Apple I admired so much in Paris & got some trees from Paris which are planted in the Kitchen Garden – *1827*

47
Wig Maker &c. &c. Mr Truefit – Bond Street Wigmaker to his Majesty – *1829*

48
Mr Hicks of Bath is the medical man there in such very high repute, it is said that he makes 10,000£ a year.
Jepsom is the man at Lymington in such a high repute. The Regent Hotel is the best.

49
Septbr. ye 3rd 1829
I bought at Mr Raws – Ipswich – the following Old Prints &c. in Suffolk – some very scarce.

No 1	Ruins of the Western Front of the Abbey Church in Bury St Edmunds, two prints	pr	2/6
No 2	Battisford, Suffolk, The Seat of Richard Foreman, Esqr		5/
No 3	Downings Map of Bury St Edmunds in 1740		3/6
No 4	Brome Hall	2 of them	5/
No 5	View in the Church Yard Bury	Plate 10 1826	2/
No 6	Guild Hall Bury	Plate 9 Do	2/
No 7	Stone Chapel Bury	Plate 8 Do	2/
No 8	Moyse Hall Bury	Plate 7 Do	2/
No 9	East Front of the Abby Gate	Plate 6 Do	2/
No 10	West Front of the Abby Gate	Plate 5 Do	2/
No 11	St Saviours Hospital	Plate 4 Do	2/
No 12	North Porch of St Marys Church	Plate 3 Do	2/
No 13	Arches at East Gate	Plate 2 Do	2/
No 14	West Front of the Saxon Tower	Plate 1 Do	2/
No 15	View of the Church of St James's, Dunwich		4/
No 16	View of Leiston Abby		4/
No 17	View of the Abby Gate of St Edmunds Bury		4/
No 18	View of Wingfield Castle, Suffolk		4/
No 19	A Perspective View of a Cottage belonging to Philip Thicknesse Esqr near Landguard Fort in Suffolk – it is now Sir Saml. Fludyers Felixstow		2/
No 20	View of the Suffolk General Hospital		
No 21	Framlingham Church		1/6
No 22	Tomb of Henry Fitzroy Duke of Richmond & Somerset in Framlingham Church		1/
No 23	Tomb of Thos. Howard Duke of Norfolk in Framlingham Church		1/
No 24	Saxted Church united with Framlingham		1/
No 25	Tomb of Henry Howard Earl of Surrey in Framlingham Church		1/
No 26	Elmset Church, Suffolk, nr. Hadleigh		1/
No 27	Benacre Hall, Suffolk		1/

No 28	Rendlesham		1/6
No 29	Mettingham Castle, Suffolk	2 prints	1/
No 30	Brightwell in the County of Suffolk		1/
No 31	Remains of the Grey Friars Monastery, Dunwich, Suffolk		1/
No 32	Sproughton Chantry		1/6
No 33	Orford, Suffolk		6
No 34	The Revd. Wm. Jones of Nayland		1/
No 35	Parsonage House at Euston, Suffolk		1/6
No 36	Tendring Hall Chaple in the Parish of Stoke the East Window		1/
No 37	Antient Funeral Monuments, Tendring		1/
No 38, 39 & 40	3 Prints of Gates of Ipswich	1/6d each	4/6
No 41	The Font in St Peters Church		1/
			£3 = 17 = 6

50

Monday the 7th of Septbr. 1829

Bought the following Prints of Mr Raw

No 42	Admiral Vernon	2 prints pr	1/6
No 43	Monuments of Bowater Vernon & Thos. Vernon		3/
No 44	Do of Edward Vernon & Richd. Vernon		3/6
No 45	Do of Thos. Vernon		3/
No 46	Honington Church & the Cottage in which Bloomfield the Poet was born	pr	1/
No 47	Honble. Wm. Rowley Esqr		2/
No 48	Mr Wollaston		2/6
No 49	Lady Elizabeth Brooke		3/6
No 50	The Duke of Grafton		4/
No 51	Thomas Gooch		4/
No 52	John Symonds		3/
No 53	Sir Thos. Allen		5/
No 54	A View near Bury, Suffolk, Mr Capel Lofft		3/6
No 55	Cardinal Wolsey		2/6
No 56	Framlingham Castle	2 prints	3/
No 57	Mrs Elizabeth Drury		3/
No 58	Henry Bunbury Esqr		5/
No 59	Woodbridge	1 print & 2 Etchings	1/6
No 60	Genl. Talmash		5/
No 61	The Right Honble. & Revd. James Cornwallis		1/6
No 62	Edward Calver		2/6
No 63	Thomas Paine		1/6
No 64	Duel between Ld. Harvey & Honble. Wm. Pulteney		3/
No 65	Mrs Trimmer		1/6

No 66	Lavenham Church	2 Prints	2/6
No 67	Butley Priory	Large Print	2/6
No 68	Framlingham Castle		2/6
No 69	Orford Chapel		1/6
No 70	Orford Castle		2/6
No 71	Southwold Cold. Print dedicated to Adml. Vernon		4/

4 = 4 = 0
3 = 17 = 6

Total £8 = 1 = 6

51
Suffolk Prints I bought of Deck, Ipswich, so much cheaper than Raw.

No 72	View of the Saxon Tower, St James's Church, the Mausoleum, the Ruins of the Abbey Church, the Hospital &c. in St Edmunds-Bury	pr	1/6
No 73	Revd. John Langston D.D. late of Ipswich		6d
No 74	Revd. Wm. Notcutt Do		6d
No 75	Revd. Charles Atkinson Ipswich		6d
	Ruins of the Western Front of the Abby Church in St Edmunds Bury	marked No 1 before	1/6
No 76	Bedericsworthe or Eadmundstow, now Bury St Edmds.		6d
No 77	The Gate of Arwerton Hall Suffolk		8d
	Framlingham Castle before marked 68		3d
No 78	A Perspective View of St Edmunds Bury Abby		1/
No 79	View at Wolverstone Suffolk painted by T. Gainsborough		6d
No 80	Fakenham from Euston Park		6d
No 81	Bedericsworthe, or Bury St Edmunds Suffolk		9d
No 82	The Temple in Euston Park		6d
No 83	Saxham Hall Suffolk the Seat of Thos. Mills Esqr.		4d
No 84	Tostock near Bury Suffolk		6d
No 85	Revd. Richard Wearing, Rendham Suffolk		6d
No 86	Revd. James Bowers late of Haverhill Suffolk		6d
No 87	Parts of the Chapel Orford Suffolk		6d
No 88	Leiston Abby Suffolk		6d
No 89	The Seat of N.L. Acton Esqr. Livermere near Bury Suffolk		4d
	Mettingham Castle Suffolk		6d
No 90	Remains of the Bishops Palace, Sudbury Suffolk		6d
No 91	Abby Gate, Bury Suffolk		6d
No 92	Charles Earl Cornwallis		2/
No 93	Euston Hall in Suffolk		4d
No 94	Troston Hall		1/
No 95	The East view in St Edmunds Bury		1/

52

Views of Bury that I bought at Bury in *August 1830*

No 96	Lithographic print of East Gate Bridge	1/
No 97	View in the Abby Grounds	1/
No 98	View in East Gate Street	1/
No 99	View from the Botanic Garden	1/
No 100	Chapel House	1/
No 101	View of Market Hall Bury St Edmunds with Market Cross &c at the commencement of the 17th Century from a Picture in the Possession of O.R. Oakes, Esqr. to whom this drawing is respectfully dedicated by his obedt. Servt. J. Ladbrooke	
No 102	Shrubland Park	3d
No 103	Orford Chapel	3d
No 104	Stowmarket Church	3d
No 105	Somerleyton Hall the Seat of the Revd. George Anguish Suffolk	3d
No 106	Euston Hall the Duke of Grafton	3d
No 107	Bishops Palace, Sudbury	3d
No 108	Rose Hall Barsham	3d
No 109	Hoxne Hall the Seat of the Honble Maynard Esqr. Suffolk	3d
No 110	Little Wenham Hall	3d
No 111	Erwarton Hall	3d
No 112	Ipswich	3d
No 113	Ringsfield Church	3d
No 114	Wingfield Castle	3d
No 115	Suffolk General Hospital	

No 116	Portrait of the late Sir Wm. Middleton a Gift
No 117	Benacre Hall
No 118	View of Southwold dedicated to Lady Rous 1820
No 119	Do dedicated to Mrs C. Acton 1826
No 120	The taking of Porto Bello by Adml. Vernon on the 22d of Novbr. 1739 his own Ship was the Burford
No 121	A View of Southwold dedicated to Sir George Crewe 1829
No 122	Samuel Kilderbee Esqr.
No 123	Arthur Gray Esqr.
No 124	Sir Charles Bunbury
No 125	Old Fuller Bury St Edmunds
No 126	Tilly Ling
No 127	Bob Martin
No 128	Harry Lee
No 129	Billy Barbrook

Billy Barbrook *Travelling Tinker*

53
March 1828
John Lund – Upholsterers' Warehouseman & Manufacturer, No.10 Mary le bone Street, St James's, London. This is the Place where Hopper bought things for outdoor Blinds &c.

54
Caldecott, 53, Great Russell Street, was the Person who by Estimate painted all the outsides of the Houses on Richmond Terrace Iron Work &c. He charged £17 = 5 = 0 for our house with the Addition of £1 = 15 = 0 for Ladders, Plaister, Cement &c. Sir Robert was very much satisfied with the Job & thought it extremely reasonable. I believe Caldecott is an Upholsterer.

55
When I was in Paris in *Septbr. 1827*, when Ld. Granville was Ambassador, Lady Granville recommended the following Milliners and Mantua Makers.

Mme. La Rochelle, Rue de Richelieu, milliners, this she employs.
Mlle. Coffy, Rue de la Ville L'Eveque, a milliner, 27 or 30.
Heil Duchoiselle, Rue Nve. des Mathurins. This is Lady Granvilles Mantua Maker & I employed her.

56
June 1830
Bought of Roberson & Miller
Manufacturers of Oil & Water Colours,
No. 51 Long Acre, London.

A small Bottle of Encre D'Or or Gold Ink price 10 shillings and a small Bottle of Encre D'Argent or Silver Ink, price 7/6. They are both of French manufacture & having only been brought to England two years ago. They may be used with a Pen or Small Sable Brush, for Ornamental Work they are the best Gold and Silver. I also bought a small Shell of Gold for 1/ to be used by just taking a little Water in your brush the same as you use Water Colours. The Sable Brushes are the best for a fine Point.
I bought at Munn's in Bond St. some Ox Gall which is good to use with your Colours for making them lay smooth.

57

I went again to 51 Long Acre to buy some tracing Paper, & Black Paper for leaving the Impression – you first take off the pattern by laying the tracing paper over. You then lay the Tracing paper on the Black & place the Black on the Silk you want to draw the pattern & by pencilling the pattern over again you leave the lines from the Black Paper on the Silk – which makes it very easy for Drawing a Pattern & very correct.

To do Poonah Painting, you lay a sheet of Horn Paper (which is made on purpose) on to the Pattern you want to take off & after having marked the Pattern with a pointed Tool made on purpose you then cut out the pattern with a Knife used for the purpose & when you have cut it out you lay it on the Silk or whatever you want to paint on & rub one of the Poonah Brushes with some Water Colour over the Pattern & when you remove the Horn Paper there is the impression left. You may use any Water Colours, it seems very easy & I was much pleased with the Man for telling me how it was done.

58

Darlington is 10 miles from Staindrop
Durham is 17 miles from Do.

To go by the Dukeries is the same distance from Newark to Doncaster.
From Newark to Ollerton – to Worksop – to Doncaster – there you come into the Road again. You must go through Clumber Park to Worksop from Ollerton.

The Road from Bury to Staindrop

From Bury to Newmarket		14 miles
To Cambridge		13
From Stanton		10
*Alconbury Hill		11
	slept there only one Inn capital	
Wansford		17
*Witham Common	a very good Inn	17
Grantham	George Inn very good	11
Newark		13
*Scarthing Moor	very good	12
*Barnby Moor	slept there only one Inn	11
Doncaster	not recommended to sleep there	14

*Ferry Bridge	The Swan is the best	15
Weatherby		17
Boroughbridge		12
*Leeming Lane		11
*Catterick Bridge		11
Staindrop		17
		226 miles

*Those marked with crosses are all excellent Inns by the side of the Road quite retired, no other Houses joining them & not in a Town.

Newcastle is 35 Miles from Staindrop & there are Ships constantly going from Ipswich to Newcastle – & there is a regular Waggon that goes backwards & forwards from Staindrop to Newcastle.
Stockton is 25 miles from Staindrop but it is cheaper to have things by Water Carriage from by Newcastle than by Stockton on account of the River dues being so expensive, & then there is no regular conveyance by land to Staindrop.

59
1830
Bath Waters are very warm & strengthening & where they agree perform wonderful cures in strengthening the Stomach. Sir George Gibbs is a Physician well thought of as an old steady Practitioner. There are two sorts of the Water one stronger than the other.

60
Fortnum & Mason, Grocers in Piccadilly, No. 182, famous for all dried fruits, & particular good hony, where Ld. Cleveland buys all his Orange Marmalade which he always eats at Breakfast which is particularly recommended to him to take by Sir Henry Halford. The Marquis drinks Seltzer Water always at dinner sometimes with a little Wine in it, sometimes without, & very often keeps the Bottle by him on the ground after dinner to drink. I hear it is the custom at Ld. Clevelands to introduce different Liqueurs between the Courses, such as Dantzick Cherry Brandy, & Whisky the Gentlemen are particularly fond of & it is thought very wholesome.

61
Garrods Hotel, Southwold
recommended by Mr Garrett who goes & stays there every year & says it is extremely comfortable & those who keep it have been servants & know what is required.

62
Underwood on Ludgate Hill, a General Shop & remarkable cheap Ribbons, Gauze Cap Ribbon very good. Mrs Merest mentioned that a Lady bought as cheap as 2d three farthings a yard this year, *1830.*

63
Hâmonieres French & English Dictry. a New Pocket one *1830.*

64

David Garrick

La premiere chose qu'on doit faire quand on a emprunté un Livre, c'est de le lire afin de pouvoir le rendre plûtôt.

The above was printed & pasted in Garrick's Books.

65
Herrings *1830*
Blown Herrings & Red Herrings may be had excellent of Mr. Atkins, Orange Merchant, Guildhall Street, Bury St Edmunds, the Blown Herrings are those that come in first, which I believe is in October. Mrs Merest has sent some blown Herrings to Ld. Cleveland for the last 3 years from Atkins & they were very good. They may also be had at Clarkes the Fishmonger at Bury.

66
Mrs Newman, Sausage Maker, Bury St Edmunds, she began making them in the middle of September.

67
Septbr. 1830
A New Van set up from Ipswich to Norwich which goes every Wednesday from the Halberd Inn Ipswich at six o'clock & returns to Ipswich every Friday Eveng. at the same hour. John Sheppard Carrier Booking Office at the Halberd.

68
Septbr. 1830
Mrs Arcedeckne recommended me to get some Foulards which are washing Silk Handkerchiefs for Cravats & Aprons, 3 will make two aprons, that is one for each front & the other cut up for a Border & 2 Pockets to each.

69
Strengtheners to take, ordered for Miss M. Martin.
Isinglass, Sugar, a little Cinnamon & Sherry – all mixed together, & a Glass full of it taken as a Strengthener once or twice in a day.
The Isinglass is boiled in some Water with a little bit of Cinnamon, then when dry, it will keep two or three days & you cut a bit of it & melt it when you want it. Whilst it is melting you add a little Sherry & Sugar or when melted. It is very pleasant & very strengthening.

Another Strengthener
The Yolk of a New laid Egg beat up with a little Sherry.

70
Poultry [*deleted*]
Mr Radish, Poulterer, Stowmarket recommended by Miss Martin as a most excellent Poulterer & reasonable. He is a very great dealer &

sends a quantity to London & Chelmsford every week. He buys up Poultry at Norwich & all round the Country. He fattens Poultry extremely well, & is famous for Geese & Turkies. He has 3 sons in the business with him.

Poultry
Mr Payne (Poulterer) Whiting Street, Bury St Edmunds.

71
Septbr. 1830
Sealing Wax 6/ a pound at Shalders, & 8/ a pound at Raws. Deck is by far the cheapest for Book Binding, & he has Pencils at a penny each.

72
Feather Beds & Mattresses
Mrs Rainer, Coddenham, near Ipswich, can new do Feather Beds & Mattresses, she can fresh Card the Wool Mattresses & new dress Feathers & wax new Tickings &c. She goes to Gentlemens Houses for 1/ a day & makes up Furniture of all sorts, Carpets, &c.

73
Wax Candles
The Candles that were ordered in *July 1829* for the Country & lasted till we went to London the 17th of March following & there were a few left.

84 lb of	Wax	short fours
6	Do.	midg. 4's
60 lb	Do.	Short threes
18	Do.	Short twelves
12 lb of Moons		
2 Do. for Lanterns		
1 lb of Bougie		
1 lb of Lampwick		
Total 184 lb		Price 30£

Lyon proposed ordering this *Summer 1830*

138 lb of Wax	Middle fours for Chandeliers & common use
24 lb Do.	Short threes for the large Candlesticks
9 lb	short twelves for Flat Candlesticks
6 lb of Moons	
1 lb of Cold. Lanterns	

1 lb of White Do
1 lb of Bougie
½ lb of Thick Lampwick
Total 180½ lb Price from 25 to 26£

30 Gallons of Oil at 7/ £14 – 2 – 0

I made an alteration in the above order. Instead of 138 lb of Wax midg. fours there were to be 50 lb of Wax middle fours &
50 lb of Composition middle fours
& no short twelves
& only 20 Gallons of Oil
The Wax Candles are 2/10d a pound
The Composition are 2/2d Do.
The latter give a small clearer light, & in the appearance you cannot perceive any difference & they burn one as long as the other.

74
Publications

The Hope of Israel, 1 Vol., recommended by Mrs Joshua Rowley, it gives an account of the North Americans to prove the Original Tribes of Israel.

Miriam, A Jewish Tale, recommended by Mrs J. Rowley, published in *1829.*

1829
Exposition of Psalm 119, as illustrative of the Character of Christian Experience. By the Revd. Charles Bridges, B.A., Vicar of Old Newton, Suffolk. I saw it at Mrs J. Rowley's.

The Undying One, a Novel written by Norton, recommended by Miss Cuthbert, *Octbr. 1830.*

The Importance of Prayer, No. 278.
The above was a Tract that a man was distributing about the Parish. London, Printed for the Religious Tract Society & sold at the Depository, 56, Paternoster Row, by J. Nisbet, 21, Berners Str., Oxford St., & by the Booksellers. Price 4/ per 100. Considerable allowance to Subscribers & Booksellers, *Septbr. 1830.*

75
A Cure for the Ague   Lady Anson
A Table spoonful of Brandy, a Table spoonful of Vinegar & a Table spoonful of Water, for a grown up Person, to be taken half an hour before the fit comes on.

76
Slack & Mortimer Jewellers
Old Bond Street (successors to Greys) where Sir Charles Vere buys things for Louisa Broke.

77
Blankets
Batly, Shopkeeper at Berghots [*Bergholt*] sells very good Blankets at five shillings a pair, yd. & 1/2 wide & 2 yds. long.

78
Parker, Warwick Street, Regent Street, for Buhl Bookcases, &c. where Calvert bought his Book Cases.

79
The Book lent to Sir Robert by Mrs Smith in *June 1830* in London, was Sir Thomas More: or Colloquies on the Progress & Prospects of Society, by Robert Southey Esq. LL.D. in 2 Vols. London, John Murray, Albemarle St 1829.

80
Nares Glossary, quarto, 1822
Printed for Robt. Triphook, Old Bond St., collection of Words & Phrases, recommended by Sir Thos. Cullum.

81
For Bronze & Brass Work of all descriptions, very reasonable,
Johnson Brooks & Hector, New Street Square, Shoe Lane, Fleet Street, London.
They make for the Great Shops, employed I believe by the Duke of Norfolk & recommended by Charles Calvert, *1830*.

82
The Daily Scripture Expositor, containing a Text of Scripture for every day in the Year with Explanatory Notes, and Brief Reflections. 3d. Edition.

Religious Tract Society, Instituted 1799.
Published & sold at the Depository, 56, Paternoster Row, by T. Nesbit, 21, Berners Street, and other Booksellers. Bound in Silk.

Daily Food for Christians.
Being a Promise, and another Scriptural Portion for every day in the Year. Together with a Verse of a Hymn. 9th Edition. Religious Tract Society as above.

The above Books were sent by Miss Fludyer to the Bazaar at Bury, *1830.*

The Journal of the Heart by Lady Charlotte Bury, recommended in 1 vol.

83
Moor Game
Directions to the Poulterer who supplies Mr Mosely with Moor Game is Mr William Simpson, Poultry Market, Edingburgh. Mr Mosely says his name may be made use of. The Sale of Moor Game is legal in Scotland. *Octbr. 24th. 1830*

84
John Croft, Cheesemonger, No. 20 Philpot Lane, Fenchurch St., London. This is the Shop we found out from an Advertisement in the Spring of 1830 & where Mrs Alloway got for us some remarkable good Westphalia Hams at 10d a lb when at the Oil Shops they were charging 16 & 18d, also Cheshire Cheese remarkably good & cheap at 6d [for] ½ a pound.

85
Fullers Transfer Varnish *1830*
for tranferring all kinds of Prints to Wood, as if the same were printed thereon.

Directions.
First take the print that is to be transferred to the wood, cut away the marginal part of the white paper then with a sponge saturate the back of it with water, but not too wet; you then take a camel-hair varnish brush and lay on a thin coat of the varnish on the face of the print, being careful that the whole is covered; you then immediately lay it down with its varnish face on the wood, and rub the same with your hand several times, being particular to observe that the Print is per-

fectly flat and that a proper adhesion has taken place, after this, you may commence to saturate the paper with water and wash it away, when you will find the whole of the impression perfectly transferred to the wood; when the same is dry take a camel-hair pencil and give it a coat of spirits of turpentine which will clear out the impression, you may then varnish it with copal spirit varnish and polish it in the usual way.

Made and sold by S. & J. Fuller at the Temple of Fancy, 34, Rathbone Place, where the greatest variety of White Wood Articles may be had, for using the Transfer Varnish, such as Cabinets, Work Boxes, Card Boxes, Face Screens, Pier Tables, Chess Boards, &c. &c. with an extensive collection of Lithographic and every kind of Modern Publication.

N.B. Varnishing done in a superior manner.

86

The Man who sells Plates of Tin or Brass for Borders, Arms, Initials &c. resembling some that belonged to the Dowager Lady Harland, lives at No. 17 Euston Place, Euston Square, his name is N. Braham & he is always ready to call when written to & brings different Borders &c. with him. They are cut in Brass I believe & you lay them on paper or any thing else & brush them over with Indian Ink – a particular short hard brush is used.

Mr Campbell of Birkfield has bought some of him this year *1830.*

87

I saw at Mr Campbells, some Partridges painted on Wood I believe, most beautifully done & more like nature than any I ever saw, also a Woodcock & Snipes. Mrs Campbell gave me the direction of the person who painted & sold them, his name is S. Taylor, 35 Rathbone Place, Oxford Street. Mr Campbell says, Taylors Puppies & Kittens are remarkably good and all his productions were much admired at some of the exhibitions. *Novbr. 1830*

88

Drawing Room Hopper *1830*

The White Ornaments in Drawing Room at Orwell are done with Paris White which is bought at the Colour Shops. You mix about three pound & a half of Paris White with a Gallon of Water & a Pint of size, and an ounce of Blue Lac or Lake I suppose. The size is made very thin with a piece of Glue about an inch square & well boiled. You add the Glue to the Water & Paris White & Blue Lac, stirring them well altogether, & then strained through a Sieve & it is fit for use.

89
1830
Housekeepers and Others taught Pastry, Confectionery, Cooking, Preserving, &c. &c. including Caramels, Wax Sugar, Chantilly and Everlasting Baskets, and every Fashionable Ornament for Table.
By T. Burford, Private Confectioner, No. 32 South Street, Manchester Square. Where may be had Moulds, Tins, Wafer Tongs and a Variety of Boards for Gum Paste, Rout Cakes, Tartlets and Pies.
London 1825. George, Printer, East Street, Manchester Square.

The above was the direction Mrs Alloway lent me to copy & where she went several times herself to take lessons in making Baskets, Rout Cakes &c. &c. in the Summer of 1830, and she has learnt to make Ices at Carters, at Burfords she was charged 5/ a lesson.

90
63 Lower Grosvenor Street, Grosvenor Square.
Mesdmes. Ruegger & Cie., Marchandes de Modes, Robes, Habits de Cour, Soyeries, Blondes & Rubans. Londres.

91
Richmond Terrace
10ft 5 Inches & a half is the width of Red Silk Curtains in Drawing Room. It scarcely touches the Ground with the Fringe at Bottom. The Curtain has not much fullness, it has a deep handsome embossed Border all round the Curtain set on rather less than an inch from the Edge, it has no Ornament at Top but draws with Large Rings on a Gilt Roller Cornice pointed at the end. A Muslin Curtain of the same size as the Silk, then they both loop back with Crimson Cords, the Curtains crossing.

92
Balls is the name of the Upholsterer in Oxford Street that we employ & one of his Men of the name of Dukes is the person that puts up & takes down the Curtains in the Drawing Rooms, & covers & uncovers the Silk Walls &c.

93
Decbr. 1830
When Sir Charles Blois was with me he told me that Mrs Harrington was the person who kept a Fish Office at Southwold, that she sells it remarkably cheap; & that if we wanted any she would convey it to Wangford to meet the Yarmouth Coach which would bring it to Ipswich. Dr Reed has it regularly twice a week in that way.

CAPT. SIR P. V. BROKE, BART R. N.

94
December 24th 1830
It has been proposed by some Farmers to have a Parish Rate to supply the poor with Coals at 6d per Bushel during the severe weather in Nacton & Levington. Sir Philip mentioned it to Sir Robt. thinking it a good plan & Sir Robt. consented to the proposal & to do what Sir Philip intended doing, so they agreed to be rated about 6d in the Pound in each Parish as Subscription, and 4£ to Levington and 10£ to Nacton as Donations to establish a fund to begin with, but not annually.
N.B. Sir Robert thinks the poor will not be so well satisfied, as when Sir Robt. & Sir Philip gave to each poor family 6 Bushel of Coals without their paying anything for it.

95
Mr Raw charged Sir Robert in *1830* £3 = 6 = 0 for 500 Farming letters which he printed for him.

96

To procure Sleep

Lady Middleton told me she found the greatest relief in taking Extract of Hops (instead of Laudanum) to make her sleep & quiet her Nerves, that it was a most excellent thing & that she had taken it by the week together, & that it could not do any harm to anyone. She takes about fifty Drops in a Glass of Water when she goes to Bed – & if necessary people may increase the quantity to 100 drops. Mr Acton had received great benefit from taking it. *Jany. 1831*

97

A warm Carriage Covering for the Feet

Lambs Wool of any Colour knitted 60 Stitches in length & about 30 in depth, then fold the knitting double & sew up the sides, & chain Stitch it over, to give it a neater look, you may draw a ribbon through the Top so that it looks like a Bag, & when you put it on the foot, one join goes in front over the Instep, & the other behind. They will not do to walk in but will easily slip on & off in a Carriage.

98

For Lumbago

1 oz of Elixir Proprietatis

½ oz of Spirits of Turpentine

½ oz of Sal Volatile – mix them in a Phial, take 56 Drops in a Wine Glass of cold water, night & morning, when the stomach is most empty.

1830 Mrs Windsors Receipt

99

Eau de Cologne

an excellent french Receipt

given me by Mrs Windsor *1830*

Put 4 Pints of Spirits of Wine at 30 degrees into a Bottle, add the following essences, shaking the Mixture 3 or 4 times a day, on the 4th day strain it through cotton Wool in a Glass funnel, always keeping the Bottle well stopped.

3/4 Drachm of Essence of Cidra

3 Drachms of Essence of Nerolay

3 Drachms of Essence of Orange

½ an oz of Bergamotte

3 Drachms of Essence of Lemon

100
Cherries in Brandy
Cut the Storks short off Morella Cherries into a Jar, & when near full, put as many quarts of Brandy as the Jar will hold & add a third of a pound of White Sugar Candy beat fine to every Quart of Brandy. Stop the Jar close & shake it to melt the Sugar. Mr Berners Receipt *1829*

101
For Ladies Work
Mrs Beecraft, embroideress, 45 Curzon Street, May Fair. Embroidery in all its variety English & Parisian executed to any pattern, & lessons, as well as for Ornamental Work given at her own or Ladies Houses & materials at the lowest rate.

102
March 1831
Miss Martin told me they bought all their Poultry of a Man of the name of John Baldwin who lives on Barham Green, about 4 miles from Ipswich. He sells very fine fat Poultry – Ducks, Chickens, Turkies, Geese, Guinea Fowls – & sends an immense quantity every week to London. He has sent as many as a hundred Geese, & 70 Turkies in a week to London. Miss M. undertook to enquire whether they would serve us when we wanted any & she says she had seen the Woman who told her she should be happy to supply us with either dead or alive. Last Sunday one son took 80 Guinea Fowls to London, & on the Tuesday they sent off 88 Fowls all picked & next week about 15th or 16th of March they will have Spring Chickens which will when picked be about the size of a Partridge. The Woman wd. send the Poultry to Ipswich. The Baldwins supply Sir Wm. & Lady Middleton in the Country & in London they have all their Poultry from them & so has Miss Martin.

A letter directed to John Baldwin, Barham Green, Claydon, will always reach them the next morning.

103
1830
Lady Martin says that the best perfume that is used is Esterhazy's Bouquet prepared by Bailey & Blews, Cockspur St., Charing Cross, London.

104
Head Ache
Malta Exotic, an excellent Remedy has been of great service to many.

105
1831
Mr Blomfield, Surgeon at Coddenham nr. Ipswich, a very clever Man, much recommended by Sir Astly Cooper, was with an Oculist 6 months to study that part of the profession, has attended all the Hospitals in London. He is always at home from 8 to 10 in the morning to see those who may call; he attends Mr Martin's family at Hemmingstone.

106
Decbr. 1830
To make Quince Jelly (The Way Louis Taitlers our French Cook made it).

Peel the Quinces, take out the Cores, & then boil them for an hour, afterwards rub them through a Sieve, then to every pint of the pulp add a pound and a quarter of Sugar. The Sugar which must be very fine Loaf is first melted in Water, & then boiled over a quick fire till, as the phrase is, it comes to a crack (so that you can break it) then add the Pulp & boil it together for an hour, & keep skimming it all the time. Apple Jelly is done in the same way.
Sir Robert says the Quince Jelly is equal to what is sold at Tours in France, which place is particularly famous for Quince Jelly.
The reason the French Preserves are so superior to the English is because they are always made with very fine Loaf Sugar which is boiled & skimmed till a pound is reduced to only a quarter of a pound, whereas the English Preserves have the pound of Sugar only reduced to 3 qrs & boiled up with the fruit, but the French boil the Sugar by itself.

107
Gloves
Duke Street, Manchester Square, the corner of Somerset St is a large shop where they sell Gentlemens Doe Skin Gloves at 1/6 a pair very good & bought by Col. Wollaston.

108
A Melting House for Plate where they will buy it of you by Weight is at Coxes, Little Britain, close to Smithfield, London. *1831*

109
Seek to be good, aim not to be great
A Womans noblest station is retreat.

110
Sermons by the late Revd. B. Scott – 1 Vol.

Goldsmiths Almanac in a Red Morocco case with Pockets, & a Spring Clasp, is what I bought for Mr Ricketts for *1832* at Decks on the Cornhill, & was much approved of.

White's History of Selbourn – very entertaining & recommended by Mr Shawe, also the Journal of a Naturalist.

111
A List of Mrs Vernon's Plate – *Jan. ye 8th 1819.*

2 Dozen & ten table Spoons
2 Dozn. Desert Spoons
2 Gravy Spoons
4 Silver Spoons
1 Soup Ladle
1 Dozn. of Tea spoons
11 Do.
2 Butter Ladles
1 Sugar do.
6 Salt Spoon, & 1 Mustard spoon
1 Marrow Spoon
2 pair of Sugar Tongs
1 Tea strainer
1 Butter Knife
3 Waiters
1 Wine Strainer
4 Wine Labels
1 Cream pail & Ladle
3 Sugar Shells
1 Punch Ladle
4 Large Candlesticks
4 small Do. & 2 Flat Candlesticks
3 Scallop Shells
1 Coffee Pot.

112
May 1831
Whilst Ld. Stair was with us he told me of an Upholsterer in Wardour Street, London of the name of Newton whom he recommended & employed himself for making Wool Mattresses in the French Way. Ld. Stair said Newton was taught by Lady Blessington & recommended by her.

113
For Rheumatism
Butlers Cajaput Opedeldoc a remarkable good remedy for the Rheumatism to rub well on the part affected.
Mrs. Windsor *Septbr. 1832*

114
Odell, Burlington Arcade, London, for Gold Lace, Cord &c. &c.

115
On a Marble Tablet in Easton Church put up by Ld. Rochford in memory of his Brother the late Mr Nassau:

Sacred to the Memory
of George Richard Savage Nassau Esqr., Brother to William Henry Fifth Earl of Rochford, and Second Son of the Honourable Richard Savage Nassau, By Ann Duchess of Hamilton and Brandon, he died the 18th of August 1823. Aged 66 Years.

Here lies a Nassau. Honour owns the name,
and George prefix'd, awakens friendship's claim.
Affection, springing from a brother's breast,
Rais'd to his worth this tributary test.
A polish'd mind, rul'd by a generous heart,
Form'd of his character the leading part;
Integrity, candour, benevolence, and Love,
on duty's course he won the glorious race,
a crown'd morality with christian grace.
Vain is the Poet's art, and Sculptor's plan,
Truth of herself best celebrates the man;
Religion guards his ashes as a prize,
And wafts his Soul immortal to the skies.

116
Farming Stock Sir Robert bought at Ld. Rochford's Sale at Easton 1831.

Diamond Mare & Foal	65 = 2 = 0
Topaz Mare & Foal	34 = 14 = 0
Ruby Mare	48 = 6 = 0
A Van	21 = 0 = 0
A Stack of Hay	84 = 0 = 0
A Chesnut Colt	19 = 8 = 6
A Cow	7 = 10 = 0
A Bull	6 = 17 = 6
	£287 = 18 = 0

117
1831 October
Lyon intended making 5 Brewings of Beer this time. He uses 9 Comb of Malt at a Brewing which makes Two Butts, & of Hops to a Bushel. The Bill for Hops in March 1831 came to 17£ – there were 70 lb at 2 shillings a pound, & 112 lb at 1/9d.

118
1831
Little Abington (Mr Charles Townleys Living) is 4 miles from Linton, 9 miles from Cambridge, 43 miles from Hemmingstone, to go by Bildeston which is 11 miles & then on to Long Melford, Clare, Haverhill. Little Abington is 52 miles from London. Thurlow is 60 miles from London.

119
October 1831 [*deleted*]
The most fashionable Milliner in London, quite the Tor, & superior to Carson, is Mdme. Croissy in Argyle Street, recommended by Lady Martin.

Miss Hicks, 19 Mount Street, Grosvenor Square, Mantua Maker, employed by Eliza Martin.

Messrs. Hodge & Lowman, (Linen Drapers & Haberdashers) Argyle House, 258 Regent Street, London, where Lady Martin buys every thing.

120
The Magazine of the Beau Monde, or Monthly Journal of Fashion, Published by T.J. Payne, No 8 Macclesfield Street, Soho, London. The above was sent me in June 1831, by Miss Carter, Pall Mall, to look at. It was No 6, Vol. 1st for June.

121
Bird Merchant at Havre
Monsr. Dumesnil, No 9 Rue de Paris, Au Havre, Vend toute espèce d'Oiseaux étrangers, singes, coquillages, cocs d'Amérique, et objets de curiosité.
The above person sells Birds to Mr Freston, Bird Merchant, at Southampton, as he told me at Havre, *July 1831.*

122
William Barker, Brazier, Tin and Iron-Plate Worker, removed from Orwell Street to Car Street, near the Salutation Inn, Ipswich.
Jobs of every description neatly & expeditiously executed.

The above is Brother to our Upper Housemaid that came from Easton, Ld. Rochfords.

123
Wedded Life in the Upper Ranks
A Novel in 2 Vols., written by Lady Isabella St. John (the Duke of Grafton's Daughter)

124
Nett Scarf *April 19th 1831.*
Mrs Metholds Scarf that she was netting had 250 Stitches in Width & 2 yds & ½ long. It was to be done, with Barber's Silk which is wound 4 or 5 times over to untwist it, or else it is so very knotty & unpleasant to work. Most excellent Barber's Silk is to be had at Goddard & Conders in the Old Butter Market, Ipswich.

The length & width of Ivory Pin is six inches & ¼ inch.

125
The Duke of Norfolk had 150 Varieties of Roses Greffées & Oeillets de Flandres Varietes 60, from Guernsey in *1831.*

ORWELL PARK,

Seat of Sir Robert Harland, Bar.t High Sheriff for the County of Suffolk.

126
Cowes
The House we lived in at Cowes was the late Mr Henry Hare Townsends House on the Watch House Quay. We took the whole House (as it is sometimes lett as a Dble. Tenement) at nine Guineas a Week from the 7th of July 1831 of Mrs Hall, House Agent, who behaved extremely well & we should apply to her again if we wanted one. Ryde is 280 miles from the Ipswich River.

127
Woodmill or Tertwood Salmon is equal to any, recommended by Adml. Wollaston, is purchased at Southampton to be had at Mr Miles, Fishmonger, High Street, Southampton, *1831.*

128
The Inn we went to at Southampton was called the Dolphin Hotel. It is kept by a woman & we were much pleased with the Accommodation we had there. White Cheddar Cheese remarkably good there. *July 1831*

129
Golden Ointment
For Inflammation of the Eyes & Eye lids, very strongly recommended by Mr Ricketts, it may be had at any one of the Chymists, it is laid on with a Camel Hair Brush & washed off with warm Water in the morning. *July 1831*

130
From London to Southampton you go by Kingston, Guildford, Farnham, Alton, Alresford, Winchester, Southampton.

131
Optician
Mr Rubingall [*Rubergall?*] Optician to the Duke of Clarence. 24 Coventry Street, Haymarket, where Miss Martin got a Pebble Glass set in Gold for her Mother to use instead of Spectacles. It looks the same as a near sighted Glass, price 33 Shillings, to be hung round the Neck with a Chain. There are Spectacles made in the same way & to wear the same. *1829*

132
Messrs. Elford, No. 65 Charing Cross, London, where we buy our common Candles. The person we first dealt with was Thomas Elford who died Decbr. 1831, but the business is carried on by his 2 Brothers, G.H. & W. Elford, Wax & Tallow Chandlers.

133
Fishmonger *Decbr. 1831*
The Person that Sir Charles Blois spoke to for supplying us with Fish is Mr Palmer, a Wholesale Butcher, and likewise a great dealer in Fish. He has sent us Cod, Haddocks, Whitings, Crimped Soles, Herrings. They are very superior to what you get in London as they come in extremely fresh.

Mr Palmer, Southwold, Suffolk.

134
A Cooling Drink.
Nitric Acid diluted, 2 Drachms 2 Ounces or two and a half of Capillaire in a quart of Spring water – Well mixed together.

135
October Brewery *1831*
Lyon made five Brewings this time. 9 Comb of Malt make 2 Butts of Beer, so we had 10 Butts brewed, which took 45 Comb of Malt.

136
October 11th 1831
Andrews & his wife came to Nacton to take the place of the Infamous Simmonss. I went to see Mrs Andrews in Novbr. & she told me there were 11 Cows in all, 3 of them had calved, but there were only 2 calves alive. 18 chickens were brought from Hundon which Mrs Andrews thinks of keeping for Stock. 4 Hens & a Cockerel & 6 little Chickens were at the Farm when Mrs A. came & since she has been here she bought 9 Chickens of Mrs Herring. Out of these 18 & 9 there are 7 Cockerels to put up to fatten. Mrs Andrews is not quite certain about the number left at the Farm, 18 young Turkies & the old Cock Turkey were brought from Burts to Mrs Andrews.

137
An Excellent Cure for Dropsy strongly recommended by Lady Stradbroke is
To chew Bohia Tea & then spit it out, not to swallow it, you may take it 3 or 4 times in the day or oftener.

138
Cholera.
Vapour or Hot air Bath
Directions for using the Bath
The Patient to be placed in Bed, the Wicker Cradle to be put over the Body and covered with the upper Bed clothing, the small end of the Tube to be put into the opening at the end of the Cradle, and then to place the Lamp which is to be used in the common way, with Spirits of Wine, and the large end of the Tube to be placed over it. By these means immediate perspiration will be produced which is considered so essential to the comfort and recovery of the Individual, in cases of Cholera, &c. *1832*

139
Cholera
Dr Newsons Prescription for the Cholera is 3 Grains of Calomel and half a grain of Opium.

140
Memorandum about Candles

Feby. 10th 1831 I ordered of Mr Field, Wax Chandler, Wigmore Street
54 lb of Composition Candles Platted Wicks
24 lb middling fours Wax
24 lb short fours Wax
Total 102 lb

In Septbr. following Lyon told me that all the Composition Candles were burnt out, & the short 4's, at which I was much displeased & told him the latter never could have been used by us & that something was wrong somewhere. 78 lbs were used in 28 Weeks. He said no one could get at them but himself & he hoped I did not suspect him. The short 4's are only used when we have company for the large Candlesticks & Branches. Also there was no doubt some quantity in hand when I wrote the order in Febry. In July 1830 were ordered

50 lb of Wax Middlg. size
24 lb of Short 3's
2 lb of Lantern Candles
50 lb of Composition platted wicks

	126 lb	price 16 =	3 = 8
Febry. 1831	102 lb	price 12 =	19 = 0
Total for the Year		£29 =	2 = 8
Novbr. 1830	Best Lamp Oil	13 =	1 = 6
1831 Do.		8 =	0 = 0

Octbr. 6th 1831

The Stock of Candles Lyon had by him were Middling fours	17 lb
Short fours (which ought to have been threes but were wrong sent)	2 & ½
Carriage Candles	2
	21 & ½

I wrote to Field the 6th of October 1831 for the following

60 lb of Composition Candles platted wicks
30 lb of Wax Candles short 3's

Lyon had written down for me to order 66 lb of Composition and 36 lb of Wax, but I did not chuse to order so many, that I might know better the Consumption for the Year.

141
Brandy Havre de Grace
Mdme _______ a very fat woman in the Rue d'Estemoville, where they sell the finest Brandy is made, mentioned to me by Dr Kilderbees daughter who had been at Havre.

142
Havres, famous for Neuchatel Cheeses and a Chymist in the Rue de Paris famous for the Jujubes Lozenges.

143
Cholera Morbus
Sir Matthew Tierneys recipe for Cholera Morbus, is Cajeputa Oil, 25 drops in a wine Glass of hot Water. If not relieved in 5 minutes, take 50 more.

Cajeputa Oil it is said saved Lady Clanricards life. I sent to Mr Richards the Chymist in St James's Street for some of it & he wrote on the Phial that the Dose was from 10 to 40 Drops & told Ainsworth it should be mixed with Cold Water. He also mentioned it as an excellent remedy for Rheumatism to rub the part affected with it, & to take two of three drops of it on a Lump of Sugar. A small Phial of Cajeput Oil was charged 7 shillings.

Butlers Cajeput Opodeldoc is much recommended for Rheumatism.

144
A Commentary upon the Holy Bible from Henry & Scott, to be had at the Religious Tract Society No 56 Paternoster Row 1831
Daily Food for Christians, Tract Society, a very small Book
Prayers for every day in the Week by a Clergyman of the Church of England, Pocket Edition.
Gems of Sacred Poetry, all small books that Henrietta Rowley had (except the Commentary) & recommended by Mrs J. Rowley, *Novbr. 1831.*

145
Madme. Croissy, a fashionable Milliner. No 5 Argyle Street at Parker & Barkers Tailors, recommended by Lady Martin & where she ordered Miss Martins Wedding Bonnet & the Sisters &c. She was a new person in London last year 1830, her charges are more moderate than most.

146
Mortimer, a Jeweller in Bond Street that Lady Martin employed & also Lady Euston & is one of the most fashionable.

147
Cowes *August 1831*

Captain Knight of the Medina Steam Boat at Southampton, that goes regularly to West Cowes & back, had a Yacht called the Lady of the Lake which he letts at 15 Guineas a week all expenses of Men &c. included. It is 42 Ton, & belonged to Col. or Mr Sheddon. Mr Coutt hired it this year.

The Duke of Gloucester Vessel, 35 Ton. Captn. Clark, Master, letts his Vessel at ten £ or ten Guineas a week in the Season. He resides at Cowes. Bob Ricketts is concerned for the Man, has advanced money to him I believe. The Yacht is to be improved against next year.

The Machinery for Water Closets for Yachts are sold at Staples & Collier, High Street, Southampton, Price 20£ *1831.*

Thomas Young, Sun Inn, Southampton, Steward of the Camilla Steam Boat that goes from Southampton to Havre twice a week. The above person told me that anything I wanted from Havre he could bring for me & gave me the above direction to him. *August 1831*

148
From Southampton to Havre in a Steam Boat you are 14 or 15 hours going. From Havre to Rouen by Land is about 60 miles. Caudebec the place between Havre & Rouen that you can sleep at, a beautiful situation, for the Inn is close to the Seine. You can return from Rouen to Havre in a Steamer & it takes about ten hours. The Views of the Borders of the Seine are quite Beautiful. The Duke D'Arcroix lives in the large Chateau on the Seine that we admired so much & with the clip't Trees in Avenues.
The chateau d'Angus Robert enquired so much about is près de Gisors, Haute Normandie il appartisont au Baron Breteuil – it then came to his only daughter Madme. de Matignon who had only one daughter that married the Duc de Montmorency. The Chateau d'Angus was supposed to have been the residence of the ancient Dukes of Normandy.

149
The Parrots we bought at Havre came from Vera Cruz, they were Vrai Amazon, the man said they were only a year & a half old & he had them out of the Nest when they were only 7 months old. When you want to take them out of the Cage you say donnez moi la Pate. The Male Birds name is Jaccon, the other the Female is called Cocote. Robert bought them in *August 1831* & gave them to me. The price for the two was near ten pound.

150
May 1831
Just published in one Vol. 8vo pr 7/6
An Enquiry after Prophetic Truth.
By Joseph Tyso – sold at Holdworth & Ball
– 18 St Pauls Church Yard

151
Scripture Revelations
concerning a Future State, 12mo pr 5/6
By Richd. Whately, D.D.
printed for B. Fellowes, Ludgate St., London

152
Court Journal *1830*
Bowsted, Newspaper Office, Parliament Street, London
Where we get our Court Journal.

153
Jersy *1831*
B. Saunders, Nursery & Seedsman, No 9 Halkett Place, St Heliers Jersey, where the Duke of Norfolk bought his Carnations, Tree Roses, &c.
Adml. Wollaston

154
Swedish Gloves to be bought at Mr Lobbs, Southampton & all sorts of French goods.

155
The 2d of March 1832, I ordered at Fields, Waxchandler, Wigmore St.

60lb of Composition Candles
30lb Do. Do. short threes.

156
A Great Sweetener of the Blood
A Desert spoonful of Extract of Ginger to a Packet of Sarsaparilla as much as will make half a Pint to be drank in the course of the day. Pour half a Pint of Boiling Water over one of these bits of Sarsaparilla over night, & add a Desert spoonful of Extract of Ginger. The Sarsaparilla is an extract done up in thin Bladder. I believe they sell it in Boxes, 24 bits in each.

157
For Rheumatism
Some Heads of Garlic put into a Bottle of Common White Wine. A Wine Glass full to be taken at Bed time.

158
Potted Beef
Take a lean piece of Beef of the best part, sprinkle over it a little Salt peter, the next day scatter a little salt over it, let it lay a few hours then dip it in water, and put it into a stew pot of Earthen ware with a bunch of sweet herbs, cover the pot with a common paste, let it stand in a slow oven 5 or 6 hours, when cold pick out all the lean, pound it in a mortar till quite fine and take from it every particle of fibre, add gradually the greatest part of the gravy with pepper and a little Salt and also pour over it clarified butter, by no means use any butter in pounding the meat. Dr Warren

159
For Rheumatism
I rub the part affected with One fourth of Spirit of Sal Ammoniac to three fourths of Sallad Oil. Some Spirit of Camphor may be added.

160
Coke, at Ipswich.
Is 18 shillings a Chaldron ready Money or 20/ if booked. Mr Goddard says it will give one fifth heat more than the Common Coal. The person to apply to for the Coke is Mr Goddard at the Gas Works, Ipswich. Canham, Common Carter, St Clements, Ipswich will take Coke from Ipswich to Woodbridge (provided he took 3 Chaldron) at 7/ a Chaln. or he would carry it on to Parham for 5/ a Chaln. more.

Feby. 1832

161
Lady Blois's Round Table from Gillows was 20 Guineas, very handsome Mahogany with french Polish, & a Green Cloth Cover, 2 Guineas, it stood in their new Sitting Room which I believe they call the Library, it could be used as a Loo Table or a small Dining Table.

Feby. 1832

162
Cholera
Mr Hope, surgeon of his Majestys Ship Canada states that in 1825 he cured 264 cases of Cholera spasmodic on board the Dolphin Hulk at Madras, without a single failure by the use of Nitrous (not Nitric) Acid, and that in August last 108 cases of Cholera occurred in four days in the Eurayalus Hulk, in the Medway, all of which he treated in the same manner with perfect success. The dose was fifteen drops of nitrous acid and ten of Laudunum, in gruel, every three or four hours.

1832

163
Barret, Toy Shop, North St. Brighton sells Clocks at 30 shillings, and with an Alarum at 35/-.

164
Hodgkinson, Linen Draper, New Bond St. sells Rich Silk Damask at 5/6 a yard.
Fletcher, Newgate Street for Flannel.
Paul, Royal Emporium opposite the Mansion House, Calico, Flannel, &c.
The above four directions were given me by Lady Stradbroke.
Feby. 1832

165
Whately on the Origin of Popish Errors, just published 1832 (recommended by Mrs Jos. Rowley).

166
James Maw, No 65 Aldermanbury, London, sells Injecting Machines in a small portable Mahogany Box, about the size of a Book with a Lock & Key very complete, price 2 guineas.
It is to be used with a Pint of Hot Water or Gruel in a Bason (as hot as you can bear your hand in) but do not use up every drop or it might create Wind. You must use Pomatum before you insert the Tube, you may set down on a Chair, & set down on the Tube having the Machine in front of you that you may yourself pump the injection out of the Bason.

167
A Good Cow ought to give nine Pints of Butter in a week, & a fairish Cow 7, so says Bart, *Jany. 5th 1831*

168
J. Mitchell, No 6 Norris St. Haymarket, London where R.H. bought a pr of Water Proof Boots at £2=18=0 the pair. *Feby. 1831*

169
Recipe for the Cholera for a strong person
60 Drops of Laudanum each
6 Grains of Calomel separate
If that fails to give relief
40 Drops of Laudanum more
Hartshorn & Water frequently taken.

170
Tincture of Rhubarb as a Stomach relief

2 Tea spoonfuls in a Wine glass of Water an hour before dinner is a great strengthener, and may be taken for a fortnight & then left off when the Stomach will have benefited by it.

An ounce of Laudanum contains about 480 Drops, it is sold at 6d an ounce, & the poor people are very much in the habit of buying half an ounce to take instead of a Dram. At Birmingham & Manchester the Chymists, one of them, will sell 20 Gallons a week.

171
From Little Abington (where Mrs Charles Townley lives) to Withersfield, 9 miles.

172
Published. A complete system of cooking for every day in the year by John Simpson, Cook to the Marquis of Buckingham. Printed for Steward, opposite Albany, Piccadilly, London 1806.

173
Egling, No 6 Wells Street, Hackney, for all sorts of worked borders.
1831

174
Sir George Sewards life, by Miss Porter, late published, in which is an Anecdote of Admiral Vernon. *April 1832*

175
Philips (late Kitchen & Philips) Cook & Confectioner, No 11 Upper Seymour St. where Miss Jane FitzGeralds Wedding Cake was made.
June 1832

176
Memorandum July 1832
Mr Gray, Mount St, London, is the person whom Mrs Vernon jobs her Carriage Horses of, at 140 Guineas a year, the Keep is included in this Sum so that there is no other expense for the Horses except on journies & then Mrs V. allows something extra per day.

177
Waller, Coach Maker, Long Acre, London, is where Mrs V. jobs her Carriages & Harness, the Chariot at 70 Guineas a year, & the Barouche at 50 Guineas a year, Harness included. New Carriages every five years, & once painted during the time. No expenses to Mrs V. of any sort for repairs &c except a pannel should be broke. A Hammercloth is included.

178
Dr Warrens Prescription for Digestion
4 Grains of Rhubarb and 2 Grains of Ginger to be made into 2 Pills, to be taken before Dinner.

179
For Cholera
20 Grains of Rhubarb
10 Grains of Ginger
mixed with 3 Tea spoonfuls of Brandy in half a glass of Peppermint Water.

180
For Cholera
2 Drops of Camphorated Spirits of Wine on a Lump of Sugar to be taken every ten minutes till medical advice can be had, Or, 20 Drops of Sal Volatile and 5 Drops of Laudanum to be given every 20 minutes. These two Prescriptions were given by an eminent Physician in London to a Lady who was going into the Country.

181
Fishmonger *1832*
Mr Weller, No 99, Bishopsgate Street, London, recommended by Mr Chles. Townley whose family had employed him for a long time & always had excellent fish at a reasonable price, it could be sent by an Ipswich Coach early enough to be dressed the same day at Orwell.

182
Meurices Hotel, Rue Rivoli *1832*
2 Hotels thrown into one & all new fitted up, mentioned by Mrs Cullum as all new fitted up, a Capital Cook & everything of the best, he had an Hotel in Rue St Honore.

Herbault, Marchand des Modes, Rue neuve St Augustin, No 8.

Madme. Camo

For Blonds & real handsome dress Pelegrines, Rue Dauphine, No 33.
Mrs Cullum

183

From Orwell to Hadleigh	15 Miles
From Hadleigh to Melford	14
From Melford to Eastry Lodge Hundon	12
Total	41 Miles

From Orwell to Copdock & Stoke	19 Miles
From Stoke to Melford	12
From Melford to Eastry Lodge Hundon	12
Total	43 Miles

From Orwell to Stowmarket	17 Miles
From Stowmarket to Bury	14
From Bury to Eastry Lodge Hundon	15
Total	46

There is a way from Hadleigh to Melford by Waldingfield which is only 12 miles, & you then leave Babergh Heath to go by Waldingfield. From Hundon to Melford by Stanstead is a very pretty road that I went with Robert in the Phaeton, but it is rather a longer way, but a very pretty Summer road.

184

Juliac, Marchand de broderies, rue des Michaullers au loin de la place de grève.

Madme. Vigneuille-Simon, Marchands de Modes, rue St George

Madme. Scott

185

Ear Trumpet

Sir Chles. Vere mentioned in a letter to Louisa Broke from London, *May 1833*, that he had been in company with a Person who was very Deaf, and was using a newly invented Ear Trumpet with which he could hear very well the conversation that was passing in a Room without its being addressed to him, by holding it to his Ear, it is not much longer than the finger & made of Ivory, they are to be bought at Weiss (Cutler) 62, Strand, London, price three Guineas & a half.

186
Stewed Peas Sir Robert's favourite way.

Cut two Cabbage Lettuces very fine & put them into the Stew pan with the Peas, put some Onion & a small quantity of Parsley & a piece of Butter about half the size of an Egg, pour some water over them & wash them well, then drain the water off well & put them over a slow Stove fire & let them for an hour for if done quicker they would burn, then mix on a plate not quite a Table spoonful of Flour & butter enough to mix the flour then put it into the Stew pan and as soon as melted put a little fine powdered Sugar, shake it up (without using the Spoon) and put it into the Dish.

187
Turtles
To be had at Mr Hornes, Mersey Tavern, Old Church Yard, Liverpool, recommended by Ld. Stair for Turtle, which Mr Horne sends in Jars every where even to Brussels, 4 Quarts for £2 = 12 = 0 which is 13 shillings a Quart, does 10 people: what Ld. Stair sent for was highly approved. The charge at the London Tavern is a Guinea a Quart. Ld. Sefton gets his Turtle at the above Place.

188
Messrs Bury & Read, (the corner of Red Lion St. opposite Queen St., London) Linen Drapers, Scotch Linen for Sheeting, recommended by Mrs Baker who has dealt there these 30 years for her employers, all their goods are of the best of the kind and the true Scotch Linen without any Cotton in it which makes it keep its colour so well. Mrs Shawe buys all her things there.

189
Steam Boats
Established from London to Rotterdam, & on to Manheim & Colmar and are it is said to be carried on to Basle in Switzerland.

190
Lodgings
No 100 Park Street, the house belongs to a Courier and his wife, who are relations of the Mr & Mrs Lord who lived Servants with Mr & Mrs James Cullum and now here in Bury he being a Nurseryman. Mrs Cullum could not recollect their name but told me she understood he was an excellent honest Courier. *1833*

191
Remedy against the Fly in Sheep.
Sulphur, Alum, and White Lead finely powdered. The Fly will not go near Alum, a pound of the mixture is enough for a score of Sheep. It is to be bought at Fitch's (Chymist) Old Butter Market, Ipswich.

192
A Book much recommended, *1832.*
The Records of a Good Mans Life, in 2 vols. by the Revd. Charles B. Tayler, M.A. Published by Smith, Elder & Co., 65 Cornhill.
Mr Taylor was Curate to Dr Drummond at Hadleigh, Mr Taylor's father was Partner with Mr Borham when he failed.

193
Chles. Calvert Esqr. Member for Southwark, died the *8th of Septr.,* 1832 at Chles. Rowley's at Leiston House near Saxmundham.

194
Baskets, *July 1832.*
Sophia Trott, Dealer in British & foreign Baskets, Nos. 363, 4, 5 Bazaar, Soho Square, London, all sorts of Baskets made to Order, foreign & English workmen employed. Where they sell the Cornucopia Baskets for Artificial flowers to hang by fire place on each side, made for Duchess of Richmond & others, they are gilt at the Frame Gilders, so the Woman told me who made them.

195
July 1833
Hodsons pale Ale, may be bought at Alfred Batsons, Merchant, Lime House London.
Letters must be Post Paid. 7/6 per dozn. in Pints or 5/6 in Bottles.
The above is Ale that is brewed for the East Indies & that Ld. Stair says is so particularly good for Bilious people, is so highly hopped & brewed in a particular way, it is only lately he discovered where it might be had & intends sending for some.

196
Guinesses Dublin Porter to be had at Dorks's, Savoy Street, Strand, London, mentioned by Ld. Stair. *July 1833*

197
Memorandum *July 1833*

Mrs Vernon told me that Genl. Vernon was buried in St Georges Parish, & she believed his Father was buried there. The Man that was Clerk when Genl. Vernon died is now living in South Audley Street, but he is not the Clerk now. This enquiry was made as I wanted to know who [*was*] the Mr Vernon that is buried in Hundon Vault.

198
Thread Mittens to be bought at Pope & Friths, Waterloo Place, London, recommended by Mrs Berners. *Novbr. 1833*

Swares (Hosier) No 1 Covent Garden, London, for Gloves & Thread Mittens, the latter will wash well, recommended by Lady Rendlesham, *Novbr. 1833.*

199
Fire Revivers
To be bought only at the Western Exchange, Bond Street, at a Counter where they sell Toys on the left hand side as you go in from Bond St. only 1/6 a hundred, recommended by Lady Rendlesham, *Novbr. 1833.*

200
The Hand measuring Wheel for measuring Land.

The Small Circle marked 8 is 8 Rods.

The large Circle
The long Hand once Round is a Mile, from one figure to another 40 Rods, & 80 Rods are a quarter of a mile so that from the figure of 8 to 2 is a qr of a Mile.

The short Hand from 12 to 1 marks one whole mile & so on like a Dial, the short hand that marks the hour marks the Mile, the long hand that marks the minutes marks the Rods, qrs. & half Miles.

From Library [I walked] to the left all round the Flower Garden to the Tower & by Sunk Fence to the Orangery & [back to] the Mansion & from thence back to the Bench by Orangery & back again is half a mile. Four times round the Flower Garden back to the Tower & Orangery home is 1 mile & 3 qrs.

Drawn & Eng[d] by T. Higham for the Excursions through Suffolk

ORWELL PARK.

The Seat of Sir R[t] Harland Bar[t]

NOTES

2 The book was in fact titled *Almack's, a Novel,* published in three volumes in 1826. Arethusa's identification of four hidden identities agrees with the Key published in the *The Literary Gazette* of 9 Dec 1826.

3 Copperas or green vitriol is ferrous (now iron II) sulphate.

9 corrected from version in 103

10 Edward Sparkhall was spirit merchant, grocer & draper. Drabbet is coarse linen fabric used for smock frocks.

13 Owen Roe later moved to Brook Street and set up as an engraver.

15 The Fitch and Starkie Bence Collections have copies of these caricatures.

21 James Peat was Saddler to His Majesty's Cavalry.

25 Howell & James were Silk Mercers.

40 Abraham Gall was the Chemist at 52 Abbey-gate Street, and Francis George Probart, Physician moved from 5 Honey Hill to the Church Yard between 1830 and 1839.

45 Bennett Odell was Gold Laceman & Sword Cutler.

47 Francis Trufitt, Hair Dresser of 1 New Bond Street.

50 No 54 The pen and ink and wash original for this etching in the Fitch Collections (S.R.O. Ipswich HD 480/18 p. 71) is inscribed: 'Sketched at Woodbridge 1811 whilst in the act of listening to a piece of Mozart's on the Piano Forte by Miss Violet, afterwards Mrs Pulham'.

No 64 Of this unsigned mezzotint printed in blue-green ink there is a copy in the British Museum Department of Prints and Drawings (ref. 1853-8-13-107). The Duel took place in Green Park in 1731, and the circumstances are related in the *D.N.B. s.v.* John, Baron Hervey of Ickworth (1696-1743).

52 No 101 This lithograph on stone is No 128 in the John Greene Collection of prints of Bury.

No 120 at B.M. is 1862-10-11-638-P.39, c.

Nos 125 to 129 See 15.

53 and 88 Humphrey Hopper, Sculptor, of Wigmore Street, Cavendish Square in 1826, worked in Suffolk also at Kentwell Hall, and provided the memorable monument for Lord Rendlesham in 1832.

58 They were visiting the Merests at Cockfield w. Staindrop, diocese of Durham.

61 Henry Garrod ran the Crown Hotel as a commercial inn and posting house.

64 This book label is illustrated and described in Brian North Lee, *British Bookplates,* David & Charles, 1979, Plate 226.

65 Peter Adkins of 39 Guildhall Street and John Clark of 31 Buttermarket, fishmonger.

81 Johnston Brookes & Co. in fact.

84 John Craft was his name.

94 Sir Philip Vere Broke, Bart. the Harland's neighbour at Broke Hall was victorious in the celebrated battle of the Shannon and the Chesapeake, 1813, and lucky to survive the severe head wound he sustained then.

114 duplicated from 45.

134 Can Arethusa have meant Citric Acid? Capillaire is an infusion of maidenhair fern or syrup of orange flower.

143 duplicated from 113.

174 *The Life of Sir Edward Seaward* by Miss Jane Porter came out in 1831. The anecdote concerns the Admiral's encounter with Don Francisco Martinez de Retez, the Governor of Portobello, Jamaica, who said that he did not consider the King of England himself equal in rank to himself, "for he is little better than a Dutchman". To this Vernon's reply was "You damned poltroon! with all your long yarn of hard names, what shall I call you? Down on your marrow-bones, you scoundrel, and beg pardon of these gentlemen, and of the King our master, or I'll kick you from Hell to Hackney!".

191 William Stevenson Fitch was Chemist, Postmaster and Antiquary, the last his ruling passion.

200 This entry on the rear endpaper comes after an index which adds nothing to make it worth transcription. Gaps supplied [ ] are where the endpaper is torn away.

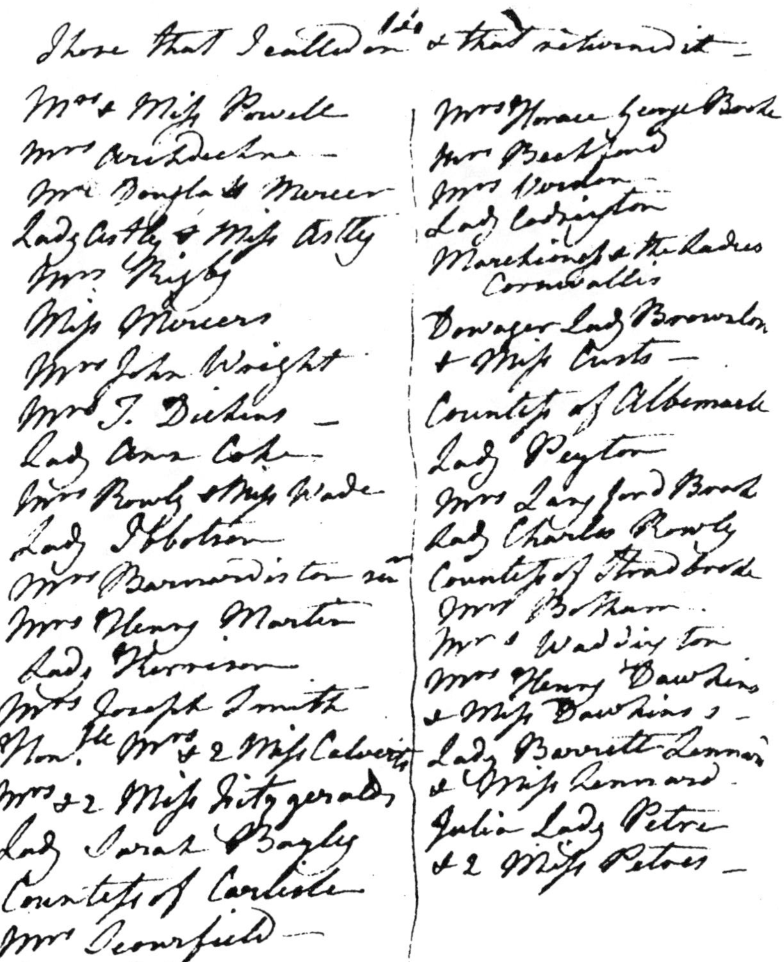

Those that I called on 1st & that returned it —

Mrs & Miss Powell
Mrs Archdeckne —
Mrs Douglas & Mercer
Lady Astley & Miss Astley
Mrs Rigby
Miss Mercers
Mrs John Wright
Mrs T. Dickins —
Lady Anne Coke —
Mrs Rowley & Miss Wade
Lady Ibbotson
Mrs Barnardiston sen[r]
Mrs Henry Martin
Lady Harrison
Mrs Joseph Smith
Hon.ble Mrs & 2 Miss Calverts
Mrs & 2 Miss Fitzgeralds
Lady Sarah Bayly
Countess of Carlisle
Mrs Greenfield —
Mrs Selwyn
Mrs Charles Calvert

Mrs Horace George Brooke
Mrs Beckford
Mrs Vernon
Lady Codrington
Marchioness & the Ladies Cornwallis
Dowager Lady Brownlow & Miss Custs —
Countess of Albemarle
Lady Peyton
Mrs Langford Brook
Lady Charles Rowley
Countess of Stradbroke
Mrs Botham
Mrs Waddington
Mrs Henry Dawkins & Miss Dawkins's —
Lady Barrett Lennard & Miss Lennard
Julia Lady Petre & 2 Miss Petres —

Facsimile of Memorandum 36, page 14 in the original manuscript.
(*Reduced 70% linear*)

Some reminiscences of Sir Robert Harland written forty years later by the Revd. Foster Barham Zincke, Vicar of Wherstead, will serve as postscript. He happened to meet Sir Robert on the day in 1848 when the Orwell Park estate was paid for. The baronet said, "There, I have in that pocket £111,000. I intend to spend the whole of it. If when I am dead and buried there is half a crown over, it will be enough". Poor Arethusa – but he did not live long enough to carry out his plan; this was the man who blamed cheque books for people's extravagances (before, he argued, they were obliged to count out each sovereign). He complained to Zincke of the heartlessness of those for whom 'he had ruined himself in entertaining and in providing with shooting' who would 'pass his door in Richmond Terrace on their way to the Houses of Parliament, and never give so much as five minutes to enliven the dull hours of an old friend'.

William Cary 1832